Richard Beck

A treatise on the construction, proper use,

And capabilities of Smith, Beck, and Beck's achromatic microscopes

Richard Beck

A treatise on the construction, proper use,
And capabilities of Smith, Beck, and Beck's achromatic microscopes

ISBN/EAN: 9783337714840

Printed in Europe, USA, Canada, Australia, Japan

Cover: Foto ©ninafisch / pixelio.de

More available books at **www.hansebooks.com**

A TREATISE

ON THE

Construction, Proper Use, and Capabilities

OF

SMITH, BECK, AND BECK'S

ACHROMATIC MICROSCOPES.

BY

RICHARD BECK.

LONDON:
PRINTED FOR SMITH, BECK, AND BECK, 31, CORNHILL:

PUBLISHED BY

JOHN VAN VOORST, PATERNOSTER ROW.

MDCCCLXV.

PRINTED BY TAYLOR AND FRANCIS,
RED LION COURT, FLEET STREET.

INTRODUCTION.

THE purpose of this work is to give, by a clear and concise description, combined with superior illustrations, the most complete directions for the use of SMITH, BECK, and BECK's Achromatic Microscopes and the accessory apparatus.

The publication has been much delayed by various causes which it is unnecessary to explain at length. It may, however, be mentioned that a considerable amount of matter is now included in the work, which it could not have contained at a much earlier issue; such, for instance, as a description of Wenham's Binocular Body, the third-class "Popular Microscope," and several new pieces of apparatus.

By giving more time than was at first intended to the preparation of this treatise, the Author has been able to allude more particularly to some of the peculiar features connected with the illumination of objects under the Microscope. Great care has also been bestowed upon the delineation of test-objects; for, preceded as this work has been by many others upon the same subject, no one has given satisfactory evidence, by illustration, of that superior performance which belongs especially to the English Microscopes.

This treatise is strictly confined to the subjects already mentioned; for although the improvement of the Microscope is intimately connected with much that has been done by its aid, it is impossible in this work to make any satisfactory reference to that wide range of observation which is so continually extending with the increase of the power of the instrument.

In concluding this introduction, the firm of SMITH, BECK, and BECK have gratefully to acknowledge the assistance they have received, whilst improving the Microscope, from the suggestions or from the contrivances of many amateurs, and especially from those of the late Mr. GEORGE JACKSON and Mr. WENHAM. But it is not with a simple mention only that any author on the Achromatic Microscope is justified in passing over the name of Mr. LISTER, all the manufacturers of the improved instrument in England being indebted to him for that theoretical and practical information at the outset, which has enabled them to advance it to its present state of perfection.

From Mr. LISTER's designs and suggestions various improvements were made in the arrangement and the appendages of the Microscope; but his attention was especially directed to the object-glasses, for the construction of which he not only determined the principle, but also recommended those combinations of lenses which, either unaltered or with modifications, are adhered to at the present day by the best makers.

From consideration for those who were engaged in the manufacture, he abstained from taking credit for these; and various misstatements since published having been allowed to pass without notice, his valuable services have lately been alluded to in a manner most superficial and erroneous.

UPPER HOLLOWAY,
March 1865.

CONTENTS.

	Page
FIRST- AND SECOND-CLASS ACHROMATIC MICROSCOPES............	1–8

Microscope-Stands; The Stage; The Mirror; The Substage; Revolving and Folding Bases; Eyepieces; Object-glasses; Universal Screw; $\frac{1}{20}$th Object-glasses.

DIRECTIONS FOR USE OF MICROSCOPE; TRANSMITTED ILLUMINATION . 8–23

The Mirror; The Diaphragm; The Achromatic Condenser; Tests for Object-glasses; Adjustment for High Powers; The Podura-scale; Methods of measuring Aperture; "Lined Objects" as Tests; Nobert's Lines; Oblique Illumination.

ILLUMINATION FROM ABOVE.............................. 23–34

Side Condensing-Lenses; Side Silver Reflector; Lieberkuhns; Forceps; Opaque Disk-revolver; Splinter of Lucifer Match; Podura-scale; Tarsus of Spider; Feather of Pigeon; *Arachnoidiscus Japonicus*.

DARK-FIELD ILLUMINATION............................... 34–36

ERECTING-GLASS FOR LOW POWER AND DISSECTION.............. 36, 37

POLARIZED LIGHT, AS APPLIED TO THE MICROSCOPE............. 37–48

Nicol's Prisms; The Selenite Plate; Darker's Retarding-plates of Selenite; Darker's Selenite Stage; Tourmalines; Polarizers for large objects; Experiments with Double-image Prisms; Crystals to show Rings.

WENHAM'S BINOCULAR BODY FOR ACHROMATIC MICROSCOPE 48–55

SUNDRY APPARATUS 55–70

Live-boxes and Trough; Screw Live-box; Lever Compressor; Wenham's Compressor; Reversible Compress-

CONTENTS.

	Page
ors; Frog Plate; Camera Lucida; Micrometers; Indicator; Double and Quadruple Nosepieces; Leeson's Goniometer; Maltwood's Finder; Microscope Lamps and Table.	
CASES FOR FIRST- AND SECOND-CLASS MICROSCOPES	70–72
THE THIRD-CLASS MICROSCOPES	73–92
The Popular Microscope; Series of Object-glasses; Description of Stand; Diaphragm; Side Condenser; Forceps; Glass Plate; Pliers; Case; Binocular Body; Mechanical Stage; Achromatic Condenser; Lieberkuhns; Dark Well; Parabolic Reflector; Polarizing Apparatus; Camera Lucida; Micrometer; Live-box; Trough; The Educational Microscope; Diaphragm; Forceps; Tray for extra Apparatus.	
THE FOURTH-CLASS MICROSCOPE. THE UNIVERSAL	93–101
Object-glasses; Eyepieces; Forceps, Pliers, and Glass Plate; Extra Apparatus and Box; Mechanical Stage; Combined Body; Binocular Body.	
SINGLE MICROSCOPES AND MAGNIFIERS	102–113
Darwin's Dissecting Microscope and Apparatus; Improved ditto, with Binocular arrangement; Patent Achromatic Binocular Magnifiers and Stand; Hand-magnifier and Stand for ditto; Coddington Lenses.	
INSTRUMENTS USED IN PREPARING OBJECTS	113–119
Knives; Points; Hooks; Needle-holder; Scissors; Forceps; Quekett's Forceps; Wood-cutting Machine.	
INSTRUMENTS AND MATERIALS USED IN MOUNTING OBJECTS	119–130
Glass and other Slips; Cutting and Writing Diamonds; Thin Glass; The Disk-cutter; Canada Balsam; Brass Table and Lamp; Page's Forceps; Deane's Medium; Farrants' Medium; Glass and other Cells; Gold Size and Asphalt; Cell-machine; Glass Cells; Labels; Small Glass Bottles; Case for Instruments and Materials.	
CABINETS AND MICROSCOPIC OBJECTS	130–134

A TREATISE

ON

ACHROMATIC MICROSCOPES.

Description of Construction.

A COMPOUND ACHROMATIC MICROSCOPE consists essentially of two parts, an object-glass and an eyepiece—so called because they are respectively near the object and the eye when the instrument is in use. The object-glass screws, and the eyepiece slides, into opposite ends of a tube termed the "body," and upon the union of the two the magnifying power depends. The microscope-stand is an arrangement for carrying the body; and is combined with a stage for holding or giving traverse to an object, and a mirror or some other provision for illumination.

Microscope-Stands.

Three microscope-stands are shown, one-third their size, in Plates II., III. & IV.; they differ from each other in construction, but the following explanations will apply to all.

B

The joint at (A) allows the body (B) to be placed in a vertical, horizontal, or any intermediate position; and for the adjustment of the focus of the object-glass, a quick motion is obtained by turning either of the large milled heads (C), a smaller one (D) giving a slow motion.

The Stage.

The stage has a ledge (F), upon which the object is most frequently merely placed, but if necessary it can be clamped by carefully bringing down the spring-piece (G); the ledge will slide up or down, and the object may be pushed sideways[*]: these are the only provisions for moving the object in the plain stage (Plate IV. fig. 2); but in the other "stages with actions" this arrangement forms the coarse adjustment,—finer movements in directions at right angles to each other being effected by the milled heads (H, I); and that part also to which the ledge is attached will rotate.

The Mirror.

The mirror (K) is flat on one side and concave on the other; it swings in a rotating semicircle (L), which will slide up and down the stem (M), or can be turned on either side.

The Substage.

As the mirror alone is insufficient for many kinds of illumination, some provision has to be made for holding various pieces of apparatus between the object and the mirror. In the first-class instruments a cylindrical fitting or "short

---

[*] In the plain stage the spring-piece (G) is almost invariably used, to supply some slight resistance, and thereby to steady the side movement of the object, which is directly dependent upon the fingers.

body" (T) is mounted perfectly true with the body, and can be moved up or down by rack and pinion connected with the milled heads (U, Plates II. & III.). In the second-class instruments a short piece of tube (Plate IV. fig. 2, R), equally true in its position as in the former case, fits by a bayonet-catch into the bottom plate of the stage; but it has no rack movement. The way in which the several pieces of apparatus fit into these substage receiving-pieces will be explained in each particular case.

Revolving and Folding Bases.

In the two first-class instruments there is a revolving fitting on the base (N), by which means the microscope can be turned round without being lifted from the table. Each of these stands can also be made exceedingly portable for their size by the application of a folding base and a removeable stage; the exact dimensions of their cases under such circumstances are specified in our priced catalogues.

The Eyepieces.

There are generally three eyepieces, distinguished by the numbers 1, 2, or 3 (see Plate V.): but it is not unusual, in the examination of many object-glasses by test-objects, to employ eyepieces of still higher power, and we then supply a No. 4 or a No. 5 in addition; the latter magnifies about twice as much as the No. 3, and the former is intermediate.

The Object-glasses.

The object-glasses (see Plate V.) are numerous, and vary in many particulars; the list of them on page 5 may therefore require a few explanations.

The "focal length" is in each instance that of a single lens magnifying the same as the object-glass.

The numbers given under " linear magnifying power " (or, as they are sometimes termed, " diameters ") must be squared, to give the superficial measurement or real increase of size. The magnifying power is increased with the same object-glass by changing the eyepiece from a lower to that of a higher power; the extreme range being from No. 1 to No. 5; and also when both the object-glass and the eyepiece are the same, by pulling out the draw-tube of the body. This tube, shown at full length in Plate II. fig. 3, serves several purposes, which will be alluded to further on; it may, however, be mentioned here, that the graduations of inches and tenths on this tube should generally be kept on the left-hand side.

The " aperture " is the measurement in degrees of the cone of light admitted by each object-glass.

The erecting-glass (Plate V. fig. 4) has a special notice at p. 36. Many particulars connected with the use of the object-glasses are supplied in other parts of this treatise; and we will only add here, in connexion with the list, that we have made most of these object-glasses for many years. The construction of some of them was for a long time peculiar to ourselves; and although both this and their nomenclature have been copied by others, we are still persuaded that the attention we give to them in every respect obtains a large amount of favour with microscopists.

Another list of object-glasses, which we term our Educational Series, is given further on, in the description of our third-class instruments.

OBJECT-GLASSES.

List of Achromatic Object-glasses.

Focal length.		Linear magnifying power nearly, with eyepieces					Degrees of angle of aperture, about
		No. 1.	No. 2.	No. 3.	No. 4.	No. 5.	
3 inches	Draw-tube closed	12	20	40	48	74	12
	Ditto if drawn out, add for each inch	2	4	6	7	10	
2 inches	Draw-tube closed	20	38	70	85	130	18
	Ditto if drawn out, add for each inch	4	6	8	12	15	
1½ inch	Draw-tube closed	30	56	100	120	190	23
	Ditto if drawn out, add for each inch	5	7	12	15	22	
⅔ inch	Draw-tube closed	70	120	220	270	410	35
	Ditto if drawn out, add for each inch	8	14	25	27	48	
4/10 inch	Draw-tube closed	120	210	370	460	710	55
	Ditto if drawn out, add for each inch	14	24	34	46	70	
4/10 inch	Draw-tube closed	146	255	460	560	890	90
	Ditto if drawn out, add for each inch	18	32	48	60	80	
¼ inch	Draw-tube closed	200	340	590	720	1120	75
	Ditto if drawn out, add for each inch	24	42	63	85	120	
⅕ inch	Draw-tube closed	225	400	700	860	1450	85
	Ditto if drawn out, add for each inch	18	35	60	80	130	
⅙ inch	Draw-tube closed	225	400	700	860	1450	100
	Ditto if drawn out, add for each inch	18	35	60	80	130	
⅛ inch	Draw-tube closed	500	870	1500	1850	2800	120
	Ditto if drawn out, add for each inch	60	100	180	190	370	
1/20 inch	Draw-tube closed	900	1570	2750	3450	4950	140
	Ditto if drawn out, add for each inch	80	150	300	350	900	

The list of magnifying powers, as given above, is only approximate; but if the exact power of any object-glass be required, it may be easily obtained in the way described at page 63.

The "Universal Screw."

All the object-glasses in both lists are made with what is called the "universal screw"—a standard size which the principal microscope-makers of England have adopted for the attachment of the object-glass to the instrument. When this uniformity of screw was proposed by the Microscopical Society of London, we immediately approved the suggestion, and also established a series of gauges connected with Whitworth's standard sizes, which have been found to answer most satisfactorily*.

The $\frac{1}{20}$th Object-glass.

The most important addition we have made of late to our object-glasses is the $\frac{1}{20}$th. This high power is constructed for the examination of those objects which require the greatest amount of amplification, but not that extreme angle of aperture which involves the employment of the very thinnest glass and the most careful preparation of the object. The $\frac{1}{20}$th will adjust through any covering-glass not more than ·005 in. thick; and, when in focus, there is sufficient space between the front lens and the object to admit of its use in the examination of ordinary preparations: under these conditions it can be employed with the same facility as an object-glass of only half the power.

In Plate XXIV. are illustrations of two objects, selected from the animal and vegetable kingdoms; these are shown as they appear under a $\frac{1}{20}$th, with the No. 1 eyepiece, the linear magnifying power being about 900 linear. Fig. 1 is the under side of the head and thorax of the *Demodex folli-*

---

* Quarterly Journal of Microscopical Science, July 1859, "Remarks on the Universal Screw." By Richard Beck. (Read May 26th, 1859.)

culorum, a minute parasite infesting the sebaceous and hair-follicles of the human skin. They are easily obtained by pressing out the contents of the follicles on the sides or bridge of the nose: if this matter be gently stirred up with a small camel's-hair pencil in a little olive oil, the parasites become disengaged, and should be removed to a small quantity of fresh oil, with a piece of thin glass placed over; and under this pressure they will retain their life and correct appearance for one or two days. The legs are very short, apparently composed of three joints, and the last one is terminated by a single claw: each leg is moved in a very deliberate manner, and describes a semicircular course at its extremity; during the backward stroke the claw is retracted, but it is jerked out again rapidly at the commencement of the forward movement.

There are two organs (A, B) at the side of the head, which are perhaps palpi; they are constantly moved up or down during life, and are apparently provided with two flaps as a means of clasping. The parts occupying the central portion of the head may represent the mandibles and a labium; but this parasite is altogether a remarkable instance of the difficulty of determining the exact organization of a transparent object. The magnifying power is abundantly sufficient for the purpose; but, owing to the refraction of the light through the denser parts, and the upper and the under surfaces being equally apparent in the thinner parts, it has only been after an examination of many specimens for several days that we have been able to determine the structure so far as it is here shown, whilst we know there is still much left in perfect obscurity.

Figs. 2 and 3 are respectively the front and profile views of the stinging-hairs from the stem of the common nettle (*Urtica dioica*). It appears at first sight somewhat surprising that these hairs, which are known to enter the skin with so slight a touch, should have a blunt bulbous extremity; but this is the very provision for the peculiar effect they produce. When any slight pressure is brought upon the extremity of the hair, the bulbous part breaks off, leaving an exceedingly sharp-cutting point (see fig. 4), admirably adapted for entering the skin, at the same time making an aperture at the extremity of the hair, from which the contents of the cell escape and enter the puncture. When the hairs are young and unbroken, a beautiful circulation is visible. Objects of this class can be examined under the $\frac{1}{50}$th with as much facility as under a $\frac{1}{8}$th; the conditions being such as to cause many high powers of large aperture to be perfectly useless.

Directions for Use of Microscope.—Management of the Light.

For general purposes the body of the microscope is inclined as shown in the Plates, but this position is varied according to circumstances.

The light should, if possible, be on the left of the observer: the best is that from a white cloud on a bright day; but a most satisfactory effect can be obtained from a wax or Palmer's candle if protected by a glass, a good oil-lamp, or an argand gas-burner, *provided they are not more than* 10 *or* 12 *inches from the microscope*: but with all the artificial means of illumination there should be some arrangement for raising or lowering the light, and for holding a shade as a protection to the eyes (see Description of Lamps).

In the examination of an object choose the object-glass that appears best suited for it, remembering that in investigation it is best to begin with the lower powers for a general view, and afterwards to ascend to the higher, which give greater detail of minute parts.

The right management of the light is indispensable for obtaining beauty of picture and fine definition, and is only to be acquired by practice; for the illumination must be varied with different objects, and often even with the same to exhibit every feature.

Every microscopic object may be said to be either transparent or opaque: this is not strictly correct, as will be seen hereafter, but the distinction is made here for the sake of division.

The Mirror.

The illumination of a transparent object is most frequently produced by reflexion from the mirror (K) below, which should generally have its centre coincident with the axis of the body. The flat side is sometimes preferable when there is abundance of light by day; but artificial light almost always requires the concave mirror to condense the light to a focus upon the object.

The Diaphragm.

With the $\frac{4}{10}$ths and lower powers the light is generally in excess, and has to be diminished by one of the smaller openings of the diaphragm (P), which is attached to the under part of the stage: its perforated plate will revolve, and each hole when central is stopped by a weak spring. If it be necessary to remove the diaphragm altogether, it will slide off at its fitting (Plate II. fig. 2, R); and the plain circular ring (S) which is then left can also be detached from its bayonet-fitting to the stage, by turning it in the direction of the arrow.

With the higher powers there is seldom too much light; but the diaphragm must often be removed altogether; and the mirror requires the most careful adjustment by its different movements, especially that by which it can be moved up or down on the stem (M), to ensure its exact focus being thrown upon the object. It must be borne in mind that by daylight the rays are parallel, and then the focus of a concave mirror will be much shorter than by an artificial light, which cannot be used advantageously at more than 10 or 12 inches from the microscope.

The Achromatic Condenser.

When the nicest illumination by the mirror fails to exhibit the structure of an object, or the best definition of an object-glass, an achromatic condenser must be employed: this is a combination of lenses by which the light is concentrated to a minute spot upon the object, without the colour and other defects which would be produced by a single lens alone. Of the two mirrors, the flat one should be invariably used; but as this gives a somewhat imperfect reflexion which interferes with the very best definition, a right-angle prism (Plate VI. fig. 4), which fits on the mirror-stem of the best instrument, is sometimes employed instead of the mirror; or the lamp may be placed at the end of the microscope, in a direct line with the body.

In the first-class instruments (Stands Nos. 1 & 2) the achromatic condenser is mounted, as shown in Plate VI. fig. 2, and fits by its tube (*a*) into the top of the cylindrical fitting (Plates II. & III., T) under the stage; in the second-class Stand, it slides by its fitting (Plate VI. fig. 1, *b*) into the short tube under the stage (Plate IV. fig. 2, R). When the achromatic condenser is in use, it must be central with the body of the microscope: this may be tested by screwing a low power on the instrument, and if the top of the condensing-lens should not appear in the centre of the field of view, the necessary movements can be made by turning the small milled heads (c, c); and these, to be convenient for use with the right hand, should be in the position shown in the drawing. The change of object-glasses involved in this plan of centering may be obviated in the first-class microscopes by sliding into the lower end of the cylindrical fitting (Plates II. & III., T), the diaphragm (Plate VI. fig. 3), when its smallest opening should appear as a bright spot in the middle of the field of view (see fig. 7). The achromatic condenser may, however, be so eccentric as to require a larger opening in the diaphragm to be used first. Or if the spot of light does not appear defined on the edge (see fig. 5), the cylindrical fitting must be moved up or down by either of the milled heads (Plates II. and III., U). The small milled heads (c, c) are used under the same circumstances as before mentioned, and full illumination is obtained by turning on the largest opening of the diaphragm.

The achromatic condenser in the second-class Stands will slide up and down in the circular ring (Plate IV. fig. 2, R); and if slightly rotated at the same time, the movement can be made very exactly. In the first-class Stands the cylinder (Plates II. & III., T) will rack up or down by turning either of the milled heads (U). This rackwork, if connected with the achromatic condenser, serves for the adjustment of its focus, which should generally be thrown upon the object. When such is the case, the image of the flame by artificial light, or of the window-bars or objects in the landscape by day, will be seen in the microscope at the same time as the object. Moving the mirror or right-angle prism will not alter the adjustments, and any particular cloud, or part of the flame, can be selected for the illumination. Another essential point is the aperture of the condensing-lenses; this is reduced from 65 to 40 degrees by removing the front lens (Plate VI. figs. 1 & 2, *d*). But in the most complete arrangement a perforated plate (fig. 6) is inserted at the back of the lenses, as shown in fig. 2; in this position it can be rotated on its axis (*e*), and the openings near its circumference can be brought in succession behind the lenses, each aperture of the plate being stopped by a slight spring when central. Five of the openings vary the aperture from 90 to 45 degrees with the front lens (*d*), and without it from 50 to 25, whilst the other three apertures cut off the rays of light in the centre and admit only those at the circumference.

Some additional instructions for the use of the achromatic condenser will be found in those parts of this treatise where the higher powers, and test-objects, are considered.

Tests for Object-glasses.

The principal points on which an object-glass has to be examined are, the spherical and chromatic aberrations, the aperture, flatness of field, and workmanship. When the term "achromatic"* is applied to an object-glass, it is inferred that all the errors consequent upon the refraction of light through its lenses are reduced to a minimum; with such a result the object-glass is called "corrected." And in connexion with the spherical and chromatic aberrations, the term "under-" or "over-corrected" is applied as the right point is exceeded or otherwise,—a single lens being regarded as "under-corrected."

* Achromatic really signifies the absence of colour only.

Spherical aberration, which is the extension of the focus of a lens, can be entirely corrected, so that an object shall appear sharp and defined in one decided plane; whilst, with a proper object, the appearance a little within, or as much beyond, the point of distinct vision will be the same.

It is impossible, so far as is yet known, entirely to correct chromatic aberration; but this aberration or separation of light into various colours, with which every one is so familiar in connexion with prisms and single lenses, can, by a proper combination of lenses, be so far counteracted as to leave only a pale green, resulting from the union of blue and yellow, which is inoffensive and quite immaterial.

Adjustment for High Powers.

In the higher powers, both of these aberrations are considerably affected by variations of the thickness in the covers of objects; for if an achromatic object-glass be corrected for an object which is completely uncovered, a piece of thin glass or any fluid, placed between the object and the object-glass, will alter that correction and produce indistinctness. It is not perceptible in the lower powers, but in the higher powers the error caused by the thinnest covering-medium becomes injurious.

To provide against this, the $\frac{4}{10}$, $\frac{1}{5}$, $\frac{1}{8}$, and $\frac{1}{20}$ object-glasses have a moveable collar divided into ten divisions (*c*) (see accompanying figure), by turning which the distance is varied between the front lens and those behind it.

When the object is uncovered, 0 on the screw-collar should stand opposite the small screw (*a*), and the line on the small piece of brass (*b*) which is let into the tube (*d*) should coincide with the line (e) engraved "uncovered": this is as far as the collar will go in that direction.

For covered objects the collar must be turned from the uncovered point, so that the numbers 1, 2, 3, &c. come in succession opposite the small screw. It is best in practice to have the object-glass on the microscope, move the collar a little at a time, focus for each alteration, and carefully watch the appearance of the object until the best definition is obtained. This mode of adjustment can be easily and very correctly made if the object be well known to the observer, or if its structure be simple and distinctly marked: the latter is peculiarly the case with the Podura-scale, and as it is easily obtained we consider it one of the very best tests.

The Podura-Scale.

The Frontispiece shows the correct appearance of a small but coarse specimen under different object-glasses with the No. 3 eyepiece; but Plate VII. more directly refers to the matter now under consideration. Each of the first six figures in this Plate represents $\frac{1}{1000}$th of an inch square, consequently the magnifying power is about 1300 linear, obtained by the $\frac{1}{8}$th object-glass and the third eyepiece. The illumination employed is that of a small lamp, close to the microscope, with its light reflected by the right-angle prism so as to pass through the achromatic condenser, which, besides being carefully centred and focused, is found to produce the best effect in this case with the smallest aperture and without the front lens. The light will be reflected most brilliantly when it is placed a little behind the right-angle prism, as shown in the annexed diagram; a being the light, b the right-angle prism, and *c* the direction of the light passing to the achromatic condenser. Good daylight will answer quite as well; and nearly the same results can be obtained with the concave mirror alone.

The drawings referred to have been very carefully made by aid of the camera lucida (the use of this piece of apparatus is described at p. 61); and whilst some size and prominence have been given to the features, great care has been taken not to exaggerate any one of the appearances.

Fig. 1 gives a representation of the markings when there are no errors in the object-glass. Its adjustment is known to be correct by the object presenting the same perfectly indistinct appearance (fig. 2) when thrown a very little either within or beyond the focus, and also, when this is done, by each marking dividing equally, somewhat as shown in fig. 3.

If the adjustment be incorrect, the appearances within and beyond the focus are never similar, but on the one side there will be strong lines (fig. 4), and on the other side a still greater indistinctness than that shown at fig. 2 (see fig. 5); whilst the best focus under such circumstances shows the markings in a general fog (fig. 6), without either the sharp black sides or the white central spot shown in fig. 1.

The exactness with which an error in adjustment can be detected is one of the best qualities of a test; and with this particular structure, using a $\frac{1}{5}$th or $\frac{1}{8}$th object-glass, a variation of $\frac{1}{1000}$th of an inch in the distance of the lenses, or about half a division on the screw-collar, can be easily detected by a practised eye.

Any chromatic aberration, as excess of colour, will be immediately seen in the light spaces between the markings of this object.

The spherical aberration should be entirely corrected so far as the adjustment by the screw-collar will work; this varies in each object-glass: thus the $\frac{4}{10}$ths has a range of about 2½ turns, equivalent to 25 divisions, and will correct for glass about ·025 thick; the ⅕th has 2 turns for glass measuring ·02; and the one turn of the ⅛th will only adjust for a thickness of ·012. Whilst on this subject, we would caution some persons against concluding that an object-glass with a moveable collar must necessarily possess an adjustment; we have seen many instances in which such an arrangement made no alteration in the correction, and other cases in which the alteration that was made exactly reversed the proper conditions. With such an object as the Podura-scale, it is not at all difficult to establish a rule for the adjustment which shall be entirely independent of the appearance presented by the object; for if, after such an adjustment as has just been made, we measure the thickness of the covering-glass, first by focusing its upper surface, which is almost sure to have dust or spots upon it, and then noticing how many divisions of the slow-motion milled head of the microscope it takes to bring the object in focus, a comparison of these divisions with those recorded in the former observation will supply the standard. As, for example, the Podura-scale shown in Plate VII. is covered with a piece of glass, and when the appearance is correct, the collar of the ⅛th object-glass is moved five divisions; and it takes six divisions on the slow-motion milled head to focus from the top to the under surface of the thin covering-glass; so that if, with the same object-glass, the cover of another object measure 9 divisions of the slow-motion milled head, 7·9 divisions must be taken on the collar of the object-glass.

If the body of the microscope be lengthened by pulling

APERTURE OF OBJECT-GLASSES.

out the draw-tube, some further correction is required for the $\frac{4}{10}$ths: thus, for 1 inch drawn out, add two divisions on the collar, for 3 inches four, and for 4 inches five divisions. The object-glasses of higher power are not so much altered by lengthening the body; but with the $\frac{1}{5}$th and $\frac{1}{8}$th, one division may be advantageously added for the first 3 inches drawn out.

In the lower powers an object should not differ in appearance, or require any alteration of focus, if moved from the centre to the edge of the field of view. This "flatness of field" is not of so much importance in the higher powers, and it is seldom obtained in them, especially when the aperture is large; but its absence the Podura-scale will show to a remarkable degree.

Aperture, as before stated, is the measurement in degrees of the cone of light admitted by the object-glass; and the definition is dependent upon it, provided the object-glass is at the same time well corrected. In the lower powers it is difficult under such conditions to exceed a certain point, whereas in the higher powers it may be said there is no limit within about 170°; but it must be remembered that the usefulness of an object-glass is destroyed when the range of adjustment, or the distance between the front of the object-glass and the object, is sacrificed to an increase of the angle of aperture. With the Podura-scale a larger aperture in the lower powers is evidenced by the mere fact of seeing the markings, and in the higher powers with the deeper eyepieces it gives a remarkable blackness and brilliancy to the picture; but, as a real test of aperture, the Podura-scale is not equal to many other objects, more especially to those siliceous valves of the Diatomaceæ which show lines under oblique illumination. After all, however, the only certain mode of ascertaining the aperture is by some mechanical means.

Methods of measuring Aperture.

Of these the simplest is that known as Mr. Wenham's, in which, by merely holding an object-glass in front of a strong light, the angle of the cone of light issuing from the front lens can be measured by means of a divided semicircular card (see Plate VI. fig. 14); but care must be taken to keep the focus of the object-glass in the centre, and also in the plane of the semicircle. This plan, however, at the best, is only intended to give a general estimate within a few degrees.

The aperture may be much more exactly measured by the instrument shown in Plate VI. fig. 12. This consists of a semicircular piece of wood about 8 inches in radius, divided into degrees on its edge (a, a), with a narrow slip of wood (f) carrying two V-pieces (b, b) turning on the centre (c). To use this, the body of the microscope (or some similar tube), with a shallow eyepiece, should be placed on the V-pieces, and there should be a small bright light in a line with the axis of the body, at a distance of about 6 feet. The object-glass to be measured is screwed on, and the point of its focus brought exactly over the centre (c); the side (d) of the narrow slip is then kept flush with the side (e) of the semicircular board, whilst the whole apparatus is moved to the right on an imaginary centre, until half of the field of view is cut off; this is the zero-point, and if the semicircular board be then kept firm and the slip (f) only be moved to the left until the field of view is again bisected, the number of degrees indicated at the point (d) will be the aperture of the object-glass.

"Lined Objects" as Tests.

"Lined objects," as such, are invariably examined by oblique illumination in a direction at right angles, or nearly so, to the lines to be observed.

Plate VII. figs. 7, 9, 10, & 12 will illustrate this by showing the various appearances of the structure of *Pleurosigma quadratum* under the different directions of illumination as indicated by the arrows. That which constitutes the test in this class of objects is the mere fact of being able to separate lines,—a power in great measure depending upon the aperture of the object-glass.

In *Navicula rhomboides* (fig. 13) the lines which appear in the direction there shown are as nearly as can be counted 75,000 to the inch (the lines and the interspaces being equal), and an object-glass of less than 120° will not separate them. The specimens, however, of the same species of the Diatomaceæ differ so considerably in the distances of their lines that none of them are equal in value as a test to the object known as Nobert's lines (Plate VIII.).

Nobert's Lines.

This is a piece of glass upon which are ruled, with the most remarkable regularity, and in a way entirely peculiar to M. Nobert, of Barth, twenty bands of minute lines; these are again divided into four sets, but from the first to the last the distance between the lines in each band is on a gradually diminishing scale of from about 13,000 to 70,000 to the inch; the particulars are given exactly on the Plate, and the number of lines in each band varies from about eight to thirty-five. The following observation may be taken as an instance of their power to test the aperture of an object-glass:—an ⅛th of 120° will show them all; but when cut down to 110° it will not separate the twentieth band, at 100° the seventeenth is the limit, at 80° the fourteenth, and at 60° the tenth.

Oblique Illumination.

The simplest way to obtain the necessary illumination for this class of observations is with the concave mirror, by turning it considerably on one side and making use of the lengthening arm (Plates II. III. & IV., W.); when this method is pushed to an extreme, the focus of the mirror must be accurately thrown upon the object, and the lamp should not be nearer than 12 inches. If the object require a still greater obliquity of illumination, it may be obtained by an Amici prism (Plate VI. fig. 11): the way in which the light passes through this is shown by the three lines (a, a', a''), and it is necessary that the prism should be so mounted that its focus may be thrown very obliquely and yet accurately upon the object (c). When in use, the mounting of the prism fits by its tube (h) into the top of the cylindrical fitting of the first-class instruments; in all the other microscopes it requires a separate stand.

The prism itself can be rotated by the small milled head (d) in the semicircle (e); and this is attached to an arm (f), sliding in a dovetail box (g), which also turns on a centre at g; so that by these movements, combined with the rack-work of the cylindrical fitting, every adjustment can be made.

With the mirror or the Amici prism the object has almost always to be rotated either more or less, so that the lines may be at right angles to the direction of the illumination: this may be obviated by using Nachet's prism (fig. 10), but

OBLIQUE ILLUMINATION.

then the obliquity of the illumination is limited; the direction the rays take in passing through this prism is shown in fig. 9, and it will there be observed that the emergent pencil (fig. 9, a) comes to a focus in the axis of the mounting, shown by the line b, c; therefore when the prism is rotated, the centering of the illumination remains the same, whilst the direction is altered. The whole piece of apparatus slides into the cylindrical fitting under the stage, the rackwork of which, in the first-class instruments, will give the requisite adjustment up or down, whilst in the second class this movement is made with the fingers, and the light must in both cases be reflected from the mirror below.

The prism, when in its place, can be rotated by means of the milled edge (fig. 10, a); it can also be taken off at a fitting at b, if the inner surface require cleaning; the other surfaces are all exposed.

When the object is transparent, and the illumination is transmitted obliquely and on one side only, it is very seldom that reliance can be placed upon the appearance as a true indication of the structure. There is a striking example of this in the change the markings of *Pleurosigma formosum* assume (Plate IX. fig. 1, A, B, C, D) when only slight variations are made in the direction of the light; and we may here state that the most correct way of viewing this peculiar structure of the Diatomaceæ is undoubtedly by illuminating with the largest aperture of the achromatic condenser very carefully centered, whilst the appearance is considerably improved, as shown in fig. 1, D, by using one of the stops (Plate VI. fig. 6, a, b, c) in the diaphragm of the condenser. Under this kind of illumination, Plate VII. fig. 11 shows the appearance of the markings on *Pleurosigma quadratum*; and the upper part of the same figure also illustrates how entirely the presence of moisture will obliterate the markings, as is very frequently the case with specimens that have been mounted for some time.

It is quite possible for an object-glass, although correct in all the points hitherto mentioned, yet to be deficient in its performance from errors in workmanship; these are very various, and the causes are often as difficult to detect; but the one most evident of all is when the surfaces of the lenses, the lenses themselves, or the brass cells in which they are mounted, are not true with each other, and the object-glass is said to be badly " centered." The Podura-scale (Plate VII.) will immediately show this fault, even if the error be small, by one side of each marking being darker than the other; and the scale should be examined in a horizontal as well as a perpendicular position, for it is quite possible that an object-glass will show the markings well in one direction and not at all in the other: the scale itself, not being flat, may produce a similar appearance to that arising from bad centering; and so also will the illumination to a certain extent, if it be not central.

While on this subject, we would add one word of caution as to the appearance of an object-glass: a small chip out of the edge of a lens, a scratch, or even a surface not thoroughly polished, does not necessarily affect the performance; whereas if an object-glass be not clean (it may have been made for some years, and may require wiping at the hands of the maker, or the front lens may have been touched only by the finger), its definition will be considerably impaired, and by many it might be most unjustly condemned. We cannot also too strongly urge upon microscopists the care required in the use of the object-glasses, as only a slight blow or a fall may in a moment make the best glass utterly worthless.

The subject of test-objects has received a large share of attention from English observers, not only from the earliest times of the microscope, but more especially during the recent improvements and up to the present day; this diligent investigation, although somewhat fruitless in itself, has been of no little aid in perfecting the instrument for those who have used it as a means of research, and we strongly recommend every microscopist to test his own instrument: if the result be satisfactory, it will enable him as a scientific observer to be accurate and confident in his deduction; or if he be only an amateur, he will pursue his recreation with pleasure and comfort.

Illumination from above.

Opaque objects require, of necessity, that the light be thrown upon them from above; but this kind of illumination is frequently employed in the examination of many specimens which are more or less transparent, and when under such circumstances the term "opaque illumination" is used, it must be remembered that, although the appearance is exactly the reverse of that produced by light transmitted from below, the real condition of the object remains unchanged.

Side Condensing-Lenses.

The "bull's-eye" condenser (Plate X. fig. 7) and the smaller condensing-lenses (figs. 9 & 10) are the simplest means of obtaining illumination from above, by merely concentrating the light to a focus and in an oblique direction upon the object; the best results, however, can only be obtained by some little care in the adjustments. When the bull's-eye is used alone for this purpose, its flat side should be next the object; and the various means by which it can be brought into position are a ball-and-socket joint at fig. 7, A, a sliding horizontal tube at B, and a movement up or down on the perpendicular rod (C).

The smaller condensing-lens (fig. 10) is shown as mounted for use with the first-class stands; it fits by a square (*a*) into either of the two holes in the limb of the best instruments (Plates II. & III.), the rod (B) slides through a pipe (C), which has a ball-and-socket movement at D, and the lens swings in the semicircle (E).

Fig. 9 shows the same lens mounted on a separate stand, with a ball-and-socket at (D), a draw-tube (F), and a sliding rod (B) carrying the lens at its extremity; this being the arrangement for the second-class instruments.

When any of the condensers are in use, the lamp should not be more than 6 or 7 inches from the object, except when two of them are combined to increase the intensity of the illumination, and then the lamp may be moved 3 or 4 inches further off, with the flat side of the bull's-eye nearly close to it, so that the light is concentrated to about the diameter of the smaller condenser, and from it to the object. This kind of illumination must necessarily be one-sided; for some purposes it may be advantageously so, in many instances it is abundantly sufficient, and for large objects it is the only method available.

Side Silver Reflector.

The light, if required, may be thrown more perpendicularly by the side silver reflector (Plate X. fig. 1); this, when in use, is generally attached by its square bar (A) to one of the holes on the right-hand side of the limb of the best instruments; it is most advantageously used when reflecting the light which has in the first instance been concentrated upon it by one of the condensers. The focus of the reflector, and therefore the right distance from the object, is a little more than an inch, and the particular position in which it may be wanted is obtained by the two ball-and-socket movements at D and E and by the sliding rod (B); the small screw (G), when tightened, will prevent the rod from turning round, which it has a tendency to do from the weight of the reflector being on one side.

For the second-class instruments the side silver reflector, with the movements just described, is mounted on a base and stem similar to that shown by fig. 9.

Lieberkuhns.

But the illumination which is the best for opaque objects, because it is not only the most brilliant, but also permits any alteration in the direction of the light, is that afforded by the Lieberkuhns; these are highly polished silver cups, sliding upon the fronts of the object-glasses, and reflecting to a focus the light thrown upon them by the mirror. They are supplied to the $\frac{1}{4}$-inch and all the lower powers (see Plate X. fig. 11); but several things are essential to their proper use. The diaphragm under the stage must be invariably removed, and neither the object nor the substance upon which it is mounted should stop any more light from the mirror than is really necessary; for although a diameter of 6 or 7 tenths of an inch may make no obstruction with the $1\frac{1}{2}$-inch Lieberkuhn, about 2 tenths is the largest size that the $\frac{1}{4}$-inch will admit of without impairing the illumination.

If the object be too small or transparent, one of the dark wells (fig. 12, A, B, C) may be used as a background; of these the largest is, of course, intended for the lowest power; and they slide into the arm of the holder (fig. 12, D), which fits by its tube (E) into the cylindrical fitting under the stage. A dark well, when in use, should be brought as close behind the object as possible; and it must also be central, or nearly so, with the body of the microscope.

The direction of the illumination, when a Lieberkuhn is used, is regulated by moving the mirror, the flat side of which is generally used by daylight, and the concave is the best for artificial light; but the most intense illumination is obtained by throwing parallel rays from the lamp upon the mirror by a condensing-lens, and the flat or concave side is in this case immaterial.

The proper illumination of an object from above requires quite as much care as the most accurate treatment of transmitted light. Very slight variations in the illumination will entirely alter appearances; and the adjustments of the higher powers require especial attention, as this mode of examining objects is often the most severe test of the performance of an object-glass.

But a feature which is peculiar to this mode of illumination is the change which almost always has to be made in the position of the object itself.

Forceps for holding Objects.

If the specimen be mounted permanently on a slip of glass, it is only capable of rotation by turning the top plate of the stage of the microscope on its fitting; and this may be quite sufficient when the object is flat, and an exact analysis of its structure is unnecessary; but if otherwise, the forceps (Plate X. fig. 6) are generally used; these fit by their pin (A) into a small socket (Plates II. III. & IV., Y) on the clamping-piece of the stage, and the object is either held between the points of the forceps at B, or it may be attached by a pin or some other means to the cork end (C), the various movements of the forceps affording in either case considerable range for varying the position of the object.

The three-pronged forceps (fig. 5) are for holding large or irregular-shaped objects, the specimen being placed between the three points A, B, and C, which are made to approach each other or spread out by sliding the piece (D) to which they are attached either up or down on the stem (E); the other movements being the same as those of the ordinary forceps (fig. 6) already described.

It will be found by trial that many of the movements of these forceps are limited, and, except for objects that require but little alteration of position, there is considerable difficulty in turning an object about quickly and with certainty under moderately high powers.

To obviate these difficulties, we have contrived a piece of apparatus termed an "opaque disk-revolver"; its construction is as follows:—

Opaque Disk-revolver.

A brass plate (Plate X. fig. 2, A), which is adapted for clamping in the ordinary way upon the stage of the microscope, has a hole through it sufficiently large for a low-power Lieberkuhn. On the right side, at B, is attached a short upright stem, which turns at its base; and at its top is another fitting, in which the arm (C) can be revolved by a milling at D. But the most important movement of all is the rotation of the small socket (E) at the extremity of the arm (C). This is accomplished by means of a fine chain which communicates with the milled head (F). The object is gummed upon a small disk (G) which fits into the socket (E), and with these arrangements, as many as five sides of a cube may be examined with perfect ease, and without disturbing the position of the object on the disk.

This fact is illustrated in Plate IX. figs. 3, 4, 5, 6, & 7, which represent the appearances of the cast skin from the head of the silkworm in five different positions, the whole of these being easily brought in succession under examination with the microscope by means of the disk-revolver just described, without moving the object from the disk or holder to which it was in this case gummed, on the side opposite to that shown in fig. 7.

To preserve those objects that are permanent, the box (Plate X. fig. 4) may be used. It will contain twenty-four disks, and, the holes in which they fit being numbered, the objects may be easily registered; the top of the box on the outside at A will also hold a paper label, and a wire fixed in the centre of the outside case of the box (B) serves as a guide when it is screwed or unscrewed to prevent the objects being rubbed off. The space between the inner and outer cases is also so arranged that, if a disk should become loose, there is no room for it to get quite free and shake about to the injury of the other specimens.

Another apparatus for keeping the disks is shown in fig. 8, and consists of a brass plate capable of holding two dozen objects; each hole is numbered, and the centre is occupied by a piece of paper as a label, which is held in its place by a brass mat and milled head. The plates may be placed one above the other, as they are kept the right distance apart by four pins at the corners; and the usual plan is to pack three plates, together with the disk-revolver, in a small mahogany box by themselves.

Each disk has a small groove on the edge to facilitate its being put on or taken off by the pliers (fig. 3), which are specially made for the purpose, as the object is not unfrequently injured when the fingers only are used.

Having now described the various means of illuminating objects (whether opaque or otherwise) from above, we would draw attention to some of the results as shown in the different illustrations.

Objects illuminated from above.—Splinter of Lucifer Match.

Plate XI. fig. 1 represents a part near the termination of an oblique fracture of a lucifer match, and shows the structure of coniferous wood. We give this illustration more for its general beauty and superiority when compared with that of a section viewed as transparent, than as any remarkable test. It exhibits, however, very strikingly the necessity of illuminating in more than one direction; for if the light be thrown in a line with the medullary rays (c), they are almost invisible. To exhibit this object, Lieberkuhn illumination is much the best, and with it there is no difficulty in showing, by one adjustment of the light, the longitudinal woody tissue, the transverse medullary rays, and the beautiful coniferous glands.

Podura-Scale.

The advantage of a one-sided illumination from above, and the extent to which it may be carried, are shown by an examination of the Podura-scale (a test already alluded to as the best for transmitted light) under a $\frac{1}{8}$th with the 3rd eyepiece. It is necessary that the object be uncovered; for, with the oblique illumination that is required under such a power, a thin glass cover is the most perfect reflector; but, without this, quite sufficient light can be obtained by means of the usual large and small condensing-lenses combined; and we have the following results with this particular object, as shown in Plate XI. fig. 2, the arrow at the left-hand side indicating the direction of the light. When the markings are at right angles to the direction of the light (A), they are illuminated on the sides furthest off; when they lie in the same direction as the light, with their narrow ends pointing to it (B), the broad ends appear like brilliant spots; but when this direction is reversed (C), the light from the points is so slight that the scales appear to have lost their markings altogether*. Now if the object were an opaque substance, this result would have been a convincing proof that the markings were depressions; but as we know it to be transparent, it follows that these particular appearances can only be produced by elevations. The continuity of the markings, which is a characteristic feature of the same object when the light is transmitted from below, is not so evident by this method, most probably for the reason that the quantity of light is much diminished when only reflected from the object; there may, however, be other causes.

Tarsus of Spider.

After the two illustrations already given, the tarsus or last joint of the leg of *Tegenaria atrica*, a large spider quite common in outhouses and buildings (Plate XII. fig. 1), may be taken as a good medium object; for it is exceedingly beautiful, and a really good test. Under a power of about 50 linear, and with a Lieberkuhn, three or four different kinds of hairs may be detected; whilst nearly all of these are again covered with the most minute corrugations or very short hairs, as shown in the surrounding figures, which are more highly magnified. This structure is more especially minute, and to

---

* The markings are shown too distinctly in fig. C.

see it clearly and well defined requires the best performance of an object-glass and the nicest management of the light. The object itself wants no preparation whatever, but care must be taken that the hairs are not broken off by careless handling; and although cast skins will often furnish sufficiently good specimens, these are generally so far injured or dirty as to make it preferable to secure a living specimen for the purpose.

Feather of Pigeon.

The illustrations on the right-hand side of Plate XII. show the structure of the barbs of a pigeon's feather, examined under illumination from above. The figures above and below give the upper and under surfaces of the vane of the feather, and the intermediate one is a section in the direction of the letters a, b, fig. 2.

According to the late Professor Quekett*, there are "at least six elements entering into the composition of a single feather: viz., primarily, the quill (I) (see accompanying figure), the shaft (K), and the vane (L, L); and, secondarily, the barbs (M), with their barbules, and the barbulettes."

Each barb consists of a central rib and two dissimilar sides (see Plate XII. figs. 2 and 4); on the under side, and in the part shown by the left-hand portion at c (fig. 3), there are a series of isolated hooks or barbules, which fasten on to the opposite portion of the adjoining barb, which will be the same as the structure at d, consisting of a number of continuous ribs with recurved edges (shown here in section), and not isolated hooks similar to the left-hand

* Trans. Micr. Soc. 1849, vol. ii. p. 25.

portion (at *c*), as they have been described by the author already mentioned.

The processes or barbulettes (*e*) on the top of one side of each barb are in some birds much more fully developed than in the Pigeon, and they are especially so in the feathers of the Owl, as described in the paper already alluded to; but instead of holding the opinion given there, that such structure is for the purpose of rendering the flight of the bird noiseless, it appears to us far more probable that these processes repel any moisture and prevent it soaking into the plumage—a provision which the Owl would more especially require as a night-flying bird, and constantly exposed to heavy dews.

Arachnoidiscus Japonicus.

Plate XIII. illustrates the results that can be obtained by Lieberkuhn illumination with $\frac{1}{4}$th-in. object-glass, and represents the *Arachnoidiscus Japonicus* in three positions. This diatom, when complete, consists of two valves connected by a transparent annular membrane, shown in the edge view at the bottom of the plate.

The inner and outer surfaces of each valve vary considerably in their appearance. For whilst externally only minute annular markings, somewhat varied at the centre, are to be detected over one general plane, as in the lower figure on the left; the structure internally, as shown by the large figure at the top, is much more striking and complicated, the material here being evidently distributed so as to furnish great strength to the valve, and yet to leave a considerable space and depth unoccupied. The following diagram (fig. 1) represents the section of a valve in which the curved upper line is the elevated portion of the inner surface; it starts from the circumference as an annular plate (*a*, *b*), from which it proceeds in numerous radii or spokes, alternately

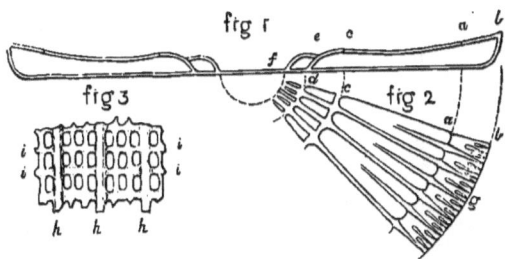

dipping down to the lower surface, or continuing to and through a smaller central annulus (*c*, *d*), which descends by a beautiful curve to the lowest surface of the valve; the radii in some specimens proceed even beyond this point, as at *e*,*f*, and the appearances (*g*) near the circumference are most probably caused by other very short perpendicular radii beneath the plate (*a*, *b*). The lower surface internally differs but little from that externally, and is shown in fig. 3 highly magnified: *h*, *h*, *h* represent the radii connected by somewhat rectangular lattice-work, in which the silex in the lines (*i*, *i*) is often of such considerable thickness as to become a distinct feature.

These particulars of structure can be easily and quickly verified by a binocular microscope, excepting perhaps the appearance shown in fig. 3, a clear view of which is dependent upon the part being quite clean and unconfused by very thick or very irregular ribs; but, with such condition, the lattice-work structure is easily detected internally, externally, or on the edge of the valve.

In endeavouring to determine the structure of any of the siliceous valves of the Diatomaceæ, it must be more particularly remembered that they consist of a transparent substance,

D

and consequently it is only the refraction or the reflexion of the light at the various edges, or irregularities of the different parts, that makes the object visible at all; it is owing to this circumstance that the dark centre of the valve has often been taken for an aperture, whereas the silex is present in this and many other parts that appear black and structureless.

"*Dark-field Illumination.*"—*Wenham's Parabola.*

An illumination which gives an appearance to objects very similar to that produced by light coming from above is the " dark-field illumination." This method of examining objects only came into general use when perfected by Mr. Wenham's invention of the parabolic reflector; but the principle itself had long been known and practised, by throwing very oblique light with the mirror.

In every kind of " dark-field illumination" the light comes upon the object from below, but at such an oblique angle as never to enter the object-glass direct; when, however, a suitable object intervenes, it disperses the light and appears in the microscope brilliantly illuminated, the field of view still remaining dark.

The action of the parabolic reflector may be easily understood by reference to Plate VI. fig. 8, which represents it in section, and shows that the rays of light, r, r', r'', entering perpendicularly at its surface (a), are reflected by its parabolic surface (b) to a focus at f, and then diverge without entering the angle cde, which may be supposed to represent the pencil of light admitted by an object-glass. To prevent any light passing through direct from the mirror, a stop (g), attached to a wire (h), is fitted in the centre, and when raised in the sliding fitting (k), it will cut off the rays which are reflected at the least angle, such as r, r'. This adjustment is necessary in cases where the object-glass has a large angle of aperture, the efficient use of the parabolic reflector being dependent upon a dark field of view.

In the first-class instruments the parabolic reflector (Plate VI. fig. 15) slides by its tube into the cylindrical fitting under the stage; and the adjustment of its focus (which is attained when its apex almost touches the object) is made by rack and pinion connected with the milled heads (Plates II. & III., U). In the other instruments it (Plate VI. fig. 13) fits into the tube (Plate IV. fig. 2, R) under the stage; and by giving it a spiral motion when in this position, that is, carefully pushing it up or down at the same time that it is turned round by the milled edge (Plate VI. fig. 13, a), the focus may be adjusted with every nicety.

As it is always necessary that the rays of light should be parallel when they enter the parabolic reflector, some care is required in the illumination. The flat mirror must always be used, and daylight has only to be reflected directly from it; but the rays from any artificial source have to be made parallel by the aid of a condensing-lens. Either the bull's-eye (Plate X. fig. 7) or small condenser on stand (fig. 9) answers well; but in using them for this purpose, whilst their distance from the mirror is immaterial, some five or six inches being best, they will only refract the rays parallel when they are placed the exact distance of their respective foci from the lamp or other source of light.

Objects for which any kind of "dark-field illumination" is available must be more or less transparent, and many which it is almost impossible to illuminate at all from above will be brilliantly shown by the parabolic reflector; the specimens will also exhibit their natural colours, which are generally quite obliterated when the light is transmitted through them in the ordinary way.

The objects we have chosen for the illustration of this subject are some of the Polycystina from the fossil Barbadoes earth (Plate XIV.), a deposit which is now universally known amongst microscopists. The drawings just alluded to, give somewhat the effect produced by illumination from above; this has only been done to give some idea of the shape of the specimens, which would otherwise appear too flat.

The Erecting-glass for reducing the magnifying power, and for Dissection.

This piece of apparatus (Plate V. fig. 4) screws into the stop at the lower end of the draw-tube, and is used in combination with the ⅔rds-inch object-glass. There are two results obtained by it: first, the object, which is always inverted by the ordinary compound microscope, is shown in its natural position, which helps considerably in dissection or when the object requires any manipulation; and, secondly, it reduces the magnifying power, but not to any one definite amount, for a very considerable range is obtained by merely sliding the draw-tube in or out, as may be seen by the following Table:—

Linear Magnifying Power of Erecting-glass, when used with the ⅔rds-inch Object-glass and No. 1 Eyepiece.

		Inches and tenths.	Mag. power.
Draw-tube pulled out		·5	5
,,	,,	·7	10
,,	,,	·0	15
,,	,,	1·15	20
,,	,,	1·55	30
,,	,,	1·95	40
,,	,,	2·35	50
,,	,,	2·8	60
,,	,,	3·2	70
,,	,,	3·6	80
,,	,,	4·	90
,,	,	4·45	100

The New Halfpenny.

To illustrate these facts we are at least successful in selecting a most familiar object, for it can only be the very richest who are not thoroughly acquainted with the new halfpenny coin of the realm; and yet, whilst this perfect knowledge of the object saves us from giving any very minute description, we venture to draw attention to one or two particulars. The coin is an exact inch in diameter (see Plate XV. figs. 2 & 3), but when magnified 5 times (about the lowest power the erecting-glass gives) it appears as seen in fig. 1, and may explain to many, in a very familiar way, what linear magnifying power really is. With the power raised to 25, the object becomes so much beyond our scope of illustration, that we have to confine ourselves to Britannia's foot alone; and we must claim the discovery of a new locality for this ubiquitous member, if henceforth, through our instrumentality, it should find place and rest in quiet microscopic cabinets.

For once we must decline a more minute microscopic examination of our object, and any further criticism we leave to those who are gifted with some knowledge of art-design or execution. On our own part we are content to point out with pride on this coin the Eddystone Lighthouse, designed and built by Smeaton, whom, originally a mathematical-instrument maker, we may honestly claim as a fellow-craftsman.

Polarized Light, as applied to the Microscope.

The use of polarized light in the microscope always produces, in suitable objects, the most beautiful effects, and it frequently assists in the accurate determination of structure when no other method is of any avail.

Nicol's Prisms.

To apply this kind of illumination to the microscope, two Nicol's prisms are generally used; and it is necessary that one, the "polarizer," should be under the object, whilst the other, the "analyzer," should be somewhere above; both prisms being mounted so that they can be turned round when in their proper positions.

In all the microscopes alluded to in these pages, the polarizer (Plate XVI. fig. 2) will slide in the fitting (fig. 1) which generally receives the diaphragm, under the stage; but in the first-class instruments it will also fit in the cylindrical fitting (as shown by fig. 22, A): it must, however, be remembered that, except when used with the achromatic condenser, as described hereafter, it is important to bring the polarizer as near as possible to the object.

The best application of the "analyzer" (fig. 4) is over the No. 1 eyepiece, in the place of the eyepiece-cap: another position for it is immediately above the object-glass, and this may be attained by either of two adapters; the one (fig. 19) screws into the stop at the lower end of the draw-tube, the other (fig. 20) forms an intermediate piece between the nose-piece of the microscope and the object-glass. In the former the analyzer cannot be rotated without turning round the draw-tube; in the latter the outside of the adapter has openings on opposite sides, so that an internal tube (fig. 20, B) which carries the prism may be easily reached by the tops of the fingers: but before the analyzer can be applied by either of these adapters, it is necessary to reduce its mountings (as shown in fig. 15), by removing the ordinary eyepiece-fitting (fig. 4, C) and the screw-cap (D).

These two positions of the analyzer may require some explanation. When the prism is placed over the eyepiece, it necessarily, from its particular shape (although made especially for the purpose), removes the eye some considerable distance from the top lens, and with all the eyepieces, except that of the lowest power, it cuts off considerable portions of the field of view: this is not the case when the analyzer is placed immediately above the object-glass, but then any defects in the workmanship of the prism (and there are sure to be some) are magnified by the eyepiece. The choice of position is therefore entirely dependent upon the character of the object; if the best definition be required, the analyzer must be used above the eyepiece, whilst the second position is often quite satisfactory to an observer who looks more at the general display than at the minute details.

The effect produced by the prisms alone may be observed by leaving one of them stationary whilst the other is turned round, and it will then be seen that twice in each revolution the light will be entirely stopped: this is, of course, supposing that an object-glass and an eyepiece are on the microscope, and that, without the prisms, there is an ordinary full illumination. If now a polarizing object, such, for instance, as that shown in Plate XVII. fig. 1 (crystals of sulphate of copper and magnesia), be placed under the microscope when the prisms stop the light, the object will present the appearance shown by the drawing, and the dark and light parts will change their relative positions when either prism is revolved: with this object, and under these conditions, no colour whatever is shown; but this deficiency may be supplied by a plate of selenite specially prepared for the purpose; for if this be put in the place of the object, the field of view will appear coloured, instead of being only black and white as with the prisms alone.

The Selenite Plate.

The particular colour given by a selenite plate is dependent upon its thickness; but each piece, during one half-revolution of either prism, will always show two distinct or, as they are termed, complementary tints, and the plates, as generally supplied, produce either red and green or blue and yellow. The colours of the selenite may be almost entirely neutralized in certain positions of the Nicol's prisms; it is therefore necessary, for varying the tint or for obtaining the greatest intensity of colour, not only to revolve either prism separately, but also to change the relative positions of both of the prisms to the selenite plate; or, what amounts to the same thing, where practicable, to rotate the selenite itself.

Either selenite plate (Plate XVI. figs. 17 or 18, the former mounted in brass, and the latter between two pieces of glass) has to be placed under the object, and does not admit of rotation; but we make provision in the first-class instruments for this movement in two ways.

In the simpler form, a circular plate of selenite (fig. 6) drops into the brass cell (fig. 8), and is held in its place by the ring (fig. 7), which fits tightly over it; the whole fitting (fig. 8) will either slide by its larger diameter (E) into the cylindrical fitting (fig. 22), or by its smaller diameter (F) it can be attached to the brass-work of the polarizer; but the milled ring (G) by which the selenite can be rotated must either project above the cylindrical fitting, or it must, as when attached to the prism, come opposite to the side opening where the finger can reach it.

Darker's Retarding-Plates of Selenite.

This other arrangement is specially contrived as the most

convenient way of using Darker's series of retarding-plates of selenite; these consist of three plates (Plate XVI. figs. 9, 10, & 11), each of them engraved on the brass rim "P|A," together with a number, $\frac{1}{4}$, $\frac{3}{4}$, or $\frac{9}{4}$, which represents a certain power of retarding a wave of polarized light. When the plates are superposed with their marks P|A in the same positions, the power they represent is the sum of their numbers; but when placed at right angles (see figs. 12 & 13), they oppose each other, and then their differences will give the power: thus if $\frac{1}{4}$ and $\frac{3}{4}$ are placed over each other with their marks P|A in the same direction, they will represent $\frac{4}{4}$; but if either of them be turned round one quarter of a revolution, they will only give $\frac{2}{4}$, and consequently the three plates, with their various alternations, will give thirteen different colours, together with their complementary tints, as shown in the following list:—

	Prisms at right angles.	Complementary tint.
$\frac{1}{4}$ by itself	very light lavender	straw-colour.
$\frac{3}{4} - \frac{1}{4} = \frac{2}{4}$	darker ditto	light yellow.
$\frac{3}{4}$ by itself	deep blue	light maize.
$\frac{3}{4} + \frac{1}{4} = \frac{4}{4}$	very light blue	orange.
$\frac{9}{4} - \frac{3}{4} - \frac{1}{4} = \frac{5}{4}$	lake	emerald green.
$\frac{9}{4} - \frac{3}{4} = \frac{6}{4}$	deep blue	bright yellow.
$\frac{9}{4} + \frac{1}{4} - \frac{3}{4} = \frac{7}{4}$	light green	light purple.
$\frac{9}{4} - \frac{1}{4} = \frac{8}{4}$	light plum-colour	pea-green.
$\frac{9}{4}$ by itself	blue-green	salmon.
$\frac{9}{4} + \frac{1}{4} = \frac{10}{4}$	green-yellow	mauve.
$\frac{9}{4} + \frac{3}{4} - \frac{1}{4} = \frac{11}{4}$	pink	light green.
$\frac{9}{4} + \frac{3}{4} = \frac{12}{4}$	light pink	deep green.
$\frac{9}{4} + \frac{3}{4} + \frac{1}{4} = \frac{13}{4}$	very light red	stone-green.

The brass-work mounting, by which the alternations just given may be made under the microscope, is shown in fig. 16;

the selenites are fitted into three cells, which can be rotated in the three separate arms (J, K, L); these arms adapt by a short dovetail (M) to the cylindrical fitting (fig. 22) under the stage; when in that position, they may be turned either in or out by means of the three nibs (N, O, P), and the finger can reach the milled rings through the opening (fig. 22, H) for the purpose of rotation. By this method any change of the selenites can be made with quickness and facility, and without interference with the position of the object, or any other arrangement.

Darker's Selenite Stage.

Darker's selenite stage (Plate XVI. fig. 14) is also a very complete piece of apparatus; the three plates (figs. 9, 10, 11), already described, drop into a ring (fig. 14, R) which can be rotated in the plate (S) by turning the small milled head (T), and an arrow upon this may be used for registering any particular amount of rotation, sixteen turns making one revolution: the only objection to this arrangement is that the object which rests on the ledge (U) must be removed at every change of selenite; but in many instances this is of no consequence.

The tints produced by the selenites are again much varied by the object: thus in Plate XVII. fig. 2, the same object as in fig. 1 is represented, but with an infinite variety of colour imparted by the interposition of a plate of selenite, which by itself, and in that particular position, gives only the blue ground, as shown round the crystal.

Then, again, there are many instances in which the use of selenite only detracts from the brilliancy and the variety of the colours of such objects as are represented by the other figures, whose appearance is entirely due to the use of the prisms only. Fig. 3 is an oblique section of rhinoceros horn; fig. 4 is a section of dried tendon of the ostrich; figs. 5 & 6 are crystallized salicine (an alkaloid from the bark of the willow), these last two drawings showing the change produced by one-quarter of a revolution of one of the prisms.

All polarized light considerably diminishes the intensity of any illumination; and although this loss may not interfere with the appearance of an object under the lower objectglasses, yet, when the magnifying power is increased, some colours are quite lost, and all are much less brilliant. This deficiency of illumination may be obviated by employing the achromatic condenser to concentrate the polarized light; and the arrangement will then be to have the polarizer at the lower and the achromatic condenser at the upper end of the cylindrical fitting (Plate XVI. fig. 22),—the selenite, if used, being placed between these two, or immediately under the object; and the smaller apertures of the condenser, without the front lens, are generally quite sufficient.

Tourmalines.

Besides Nicol's prisms, there are many other means of polarizing light; of these the most remarkable are tourmalines (Plate XVI. fig. 5). Very thin slices of some of these crystals are sufficient for the purpose, and consequently as analyzers they have a great advantage over Nicol's prism in giving a full field when used above any of the eyepieces. Their only fault is that they are never free from some colour in themselves, and therefore they make material changes in the true appearance of an object. They are, moreover, when of a sufficiently light tint and still retaining their polarizing power, very scarce; so that the small pieces even, which are quite large enough for the microscope, can only be purchased at high prices.

Polarizers for large objects.

Before the extra large polarizer (Plate XVI. fig. 3) was introduced, the illumination of the whole of an object under a low power was often found to be imperfect, and was remedied by the use of some other polarizer: either a piece of black glass (fig. 21) was placed over the mirror and then inclined at the proper angle, or a bundle of thin glass plates (fig. 23), properly mounted, was slid into the cylindrical fitting under the stage, so that the light would be polarized by either passing through or by reflexion from it; but these methods are not much employed at the present time.

Experiments with Double-image Prisms.

The microscope may also be made to exhibit various results produced by polarized light, as the subjoined extract from a paper by Mr. Legg[*] may explain:—

" The following experiments, if carefully performed, will illustrate the most striking phenomena of double refraction, and form a useful introduction to the practical application of this principle.

" The apparatus necessary is—

" A Nicol's prism (Plate XVI. figs. 2 or 3) to be adapted under the stage.

" A selenite plate, figs. 17 or 18.

" Two double-refracting prisms, adapting to each other and to the eyepieces, figs. 24 and 26.

" A film of selenite adapted to the double-refracting prisms, fig. 25; and

---

[*] " On the Application of Polarized Light in Microscopic Investigations." By M. S. Legg. Read before the Microscopical Society of London, Dec. 9, 1846.

"A plate of brass, 3 inches by 1, perforated with a series of holes, fig. 27.

"*Exp.* 1.—Place the piece of brass so as for the smallest hole to be in the centre of the stage of the instrument, employing a low-power object-glass, and adjust the focus as for an ordinary microscopic object; place one double-refracting prism in the place of the cap of the eyepiece, and there will appear two distinct images (Plate XVIII. fig. 1, *a*); then by revolving the prism the images will describe a circle, the circumference of which cuts the centre of the field of view; the one is called the ordinary, and the other the extraordinary ray. By passing the slide along so as for the larger orifices to appear in the field, the images will not be completely separated, but will overlap, as in fig. 1, *b*.

"*Exp.* 2.—Place the polarizer (Plate XVI. figs. 2 or 3) into its place under the stage, still retaining the double-image prism over the eyepiece; then by examining the object there will appear in some positions two, but in others only one image; and it will be observed that at 90° from the latter position this ray will be cut off, and that which was first observed will become visible; at 180°, or one-half of the circle, an alternate change will take place; at 270° another change; and at 360°, or the completion of the circle, the original appearance (see Plate XVIII. fig. 3).

"Before proceeding to the next experiment, it will be as well to observe the position of the Nicol's prism used as a polarizer, which should be adjusted with its acute angles parallel with the sides of the stage (see fig. 7), in order to secure the greatest brilliancy in the experiment: the proper relative position of the selenite may be determined by noticing the natural fractures or flaws in the film, which will be observed to run parallel to one another: these flaws should be adjusted to about 45° from the sides of the stage, to obtain the greatest amount of depolarization (see fig. 8).

"*Exp.* 3.—If we now take the plate of selenite thus prepared, and place it under the piece of brass on the stage, we shall see, instead of the alternate white and black images, two coloured images, as in fig. 2, *c*, and fig. 4, composed of the constituents of white light, which will alternately change (by revolving the double-image prism over the eyepiece) at every quarter of the circle; then by passing the plate of brass along, so as to bring the larger orifices in succession into the field, the images will overlap, and where they overlap, white light will be produced (see fig. 2, *d*). If by accident the prism should be placed at 45° from the position just indicated (see fig. 9), no particular colour will be observed, and it will then illustrate the phenomenon of the neutral axis of selenite; because when placed in that relative position, no depolarization takes place.

"The phenomena of polarized light may be further illustrated by the addition of the second double refractor (fig. 26, Plate XVI.) and the film of selenite (fig. 25) between the double refractors.

"*Exp.* 4.—By placing the apparatus as described in the first experiment (that is, removing the Nicol's prism and plate of selenite, but retaining the brass plate), we shall observe the two images as shown in fig. 3, Plate XVIII.; then by placing the second double refractor over the first, so as for all the faces of the one to be parallel to all the faces of the other, as if they formed but one piece, the eye will perceive two distinct images, but at twice the original distance from each other (see fig. 5, *e*). If we now turn the prism nearest the eye from left to right, two faint images will appear; continuing the turn, at 45° the four images will be all equally luminous (fig. 5, f); and when the prism has turned round 90°, there will be only two images of equal brightness (fig. 5, g); continuing the turn, two other faint images will appear; further on the four images will be equal; still further they will be unequal; and at 180° of revolution they will all coalesce into one bright image (fig. 5, h).

"*Exp.* 5.—The above results will be rendered more interesting by interposing between the double refractors the film of selenite. Instead of the two white images, as in the preceding experiment, we shall see three, of which the two outer ones will be one colour (say green), and the middle, its complementary colour or red (fig. 6, i); by turning the prism nearest the eye, the middle image will gradually divide, until the completion of a quarter revolution, when four images will appear of equal brilliancy, two of each colour (fig. 6, k): revolve the prism until the completion of the half-circle, and the three images will reappear, but with different properties, the outer images being red and the middle green (fig. 6, l); at another quarter revolution, four images, but with opposite colours, will be observed (fig. 6, m), and at the completion of the revolution the original appearance (see fig. 6, i).

"In this experiment the relative positions of the double-refracting prisms and the selenite must be carefully observed, as, if the neutral axis of the selenite be parallel or perpendicular to the plane of polarization, no depolarization takes place, and no colours will be produced, the results then appearing as if the selenite were not interposed."

Crystals to show Rings.

The systems of coloured rings, produced by crystals cut perpendicularly to their axes, can also be beautifully shown in the microscope with polarized light; they are best seen by placing the polarizer (Plate XVI. figs. 2 or 3) under the stage, and employing a low-power object-glass; it is usual to place the crystal over a No. 2 eyepiece, made without a stop; and either a short prism or a tourmaline may be used as an analyzer over the crystal. Plate XVIII. fig. 10 shows the appearance of calc-spar under such circumstances.

The following is a list of the most interesting specimens, each of which is generally mounted in a brass fitting, as shown in Plate XVI. fig. 28.

List of Crystals.

Quartz, right-handed.	Nitre.
Quartz, left-handed.	Topaz.
Calc-spar.	Sugar.
Borax.	Arragonite.

Wenham's Binocular Microscope.

Wenham's binocular microscope is now so well known, that it may appear hardly necessary to occupy a portion of these pages with any explanation or defence of its principle; but binocular vision itself, as well as this particular application of it, still meets with such strong opposition from many microscopists, that we venture to give with some minuteness a few facts connected with the subject, and, more especially, because we consider Wenham's binocular body to be the most valuable addition to the compound microscope since the perfecting of the object-glasses by Mr. Lister.

That binocular vision is advantageous, if not necessary, is quite sufficiently proved by the fact of our having two eyes, and it is also known that the stereoscopic effect conveyed to the mind increases as the object approaches the eyes; consequently, when the simple design of the microscope is to enable the eyes to see an object, or the image of an object, at a shorter distance than the natural limit, under such circumstances stereoscopic vision must be of the greatest importance.

In Mr. Wenham's contrivance, the binocular body is merely an addition; when adapted to an instrument, it does not interfere in any way with the use of the single body only, in its perfect condition. This is a most important feature; for it also affords the opportunity of an immediate comparison between the appearances seen by single or double vision; and thus not only can the accuracy of the binocular body be easily tested, but the observer may obtain in an instant a double analysis of the structure or condition of an object.

We believe most of the opponents of the binocular principle to be those observers who have accustomed themselves to the examination of objects as transparent; and we venture to draw especial attention to this particular condition, under which so many judge of the value of the Binocular Microscope. This method of examination, peculiar to the microscope, and one to which the naked eye is quite unaccustomed, conveys to the mind a most imperfect idea of the form or vertical distance of the various parts of an object, whilst in very many instances the appearances bear no resemblance even in shape to the true structure: this may be readily conjectured from the various shapes the markings on *Pleurosigma formosum* assume when illuminated in different directions (see Plate IX. fig. 1); but most conclusive evidence is furnished by a careful examination of the scales of *Lepisma saccharina*.

This insect may be found in most old houses, frequenting damp, warm cupboards, or as an associate of black beetles and cockroaches, and its scales have long been known to microscopists. The insect, which is very active, may be caught without injury in a clean pill-box, with a few pin-holes in the lid; and a drop of chloroform over these holes will soon make the inmate insensible, when it may be turned out upon a piece of clean paper.

The best way to remove the scales is to press gently one of the ordinary 3×1 glass slides upon the part from which the scales are required, and they readily adhere to the glass, appearing to the naked eye like a smear of dust; under the microscope they present considerable variety, not only of size and shape, but also in the character of their markings. The scales that are most abundant resemble the one shown in Plate XIX. fig. 3, and upon it the more prominent markings appear as a series of double lines which run parallel and at considerable intervals from end to end of the scale, whilst other lines, generally much fainter, radiate from the quill and take the same direction as the outline of the scale when near the fixed or quill end; but there is in addition an interrupted appearance at the sides of the scale, which is very different from the mere union or "cross-hatching" of the two sets of lines.

In the first place, the scales themselves are truly transparent objects; for water instantly and almost entirely obliterates their markings, but they reappear unaltered as the moisture leaves them; therefore the fact of their being visible at all is due to the refraction of light by superficial irregularities.

The following experiment establishes the fact still more conclusively, and also determines the structure of each side of the scale, a matter which it is impossible to do from the appearance of the markings in their unaltered state.

Having removed some scales from the insect to a glass

slide as already described, cover them with a piece of thin glass, which may be prevented from moving by a little paste at each corner. The subjoined drawing may be taken as an exaggerated section of the various parts.

A, B, is the glass slide with scales, c, c, closely adherent to it, and D the thin glass cover secured to A, B, by a very little paste at the corners: in this state the whole should be placed under the microscope,—a high power, such as a $\frac{1}{8}$th and No. 3 eyepiece with achromatic condenser illumination, answering well. If under these circumstances a small drop of water, E, be placed at the edge of the thin glass, it will run under by capillary attraction; but when it reaches one of the scales, it will run first between it and the glass slip A, B, because the attraction there will be greater, and consequently the markings on that side of the scale which is in contact with the glass slip will be obliterated, whilst those on the other side will, for some time at least, remain unaltered; when such is the case, the strongly marked vertical lines disappear and the radiating ones become continuous (see Plate XIX. fig. 4, left-hand lower portion). To try the same experiment with the other, or inner, surface of the scales, it is only requisite to transfer them by pressing the first piece of glass, by which they are taken from the insect, upon another piece of glass, to which a few scales will adhere; and then the same process of introducing fluid, as already described, may be repeated with them, when the radiating lines will disappear and the vertical ones will become continuous (see fig. 4, right-hand side of scale). These results show, therefore, that the interrupted appearance is produced by two sets of uninterrupted lines on different surfaces.

It may be interesting to many to try these experiments for themselves, whilst others may be satisfied with the appearance which some scales are almost sure to present in every slide that is mounted. Fig. 4, already alluded to, is a camera-lucida drawing of a scale which happens to have the opposite surfaces obliterated on either side: this is seldom the case, for it is generally only the outer surface of the scale that is in such a condition.

Fig. 1 shows a small scale in a dry and natural state, the direction of the markings upon which is shown by the faint lines: at the upper part (*a*) the interrupted appearance is not much unlike that seen at the sides of the larger scales; but lower down, at *b*, where the lines are of equal strength and cross nearly at right angles, they are entirely lost in a series of dots; and exactly the same appearance is shown in fig. 2 to be produced by two scales at the part (*c*) where they overlie each other, although by themselves they only show the parallel vertical lines.

These kinds of contradictory results produced by the refraction of light, combined with an illumination to which the naked eye is unaccustomed, make the binocular microscope of little avail in the examination of true transparent objects; but with those specimens that are opaque, or nearly so, its assistance is most remarkable, and we do not know a single object of this class in which its use is not essential.

Construction of Binocular Microscope.

The only plan for a binocular microscope, as yet known to be practicable, is the equal division of the rays after they have passed through the object-glass, so that each eye may be furnished with an appropriate one-sided view of the object. The methods at first contrived to effect this not only materially injured the definition of the object-glasses, but also required expensive alterations in their adaptation, or more frequently still a separate stand; whereas the following arrangement, contrived by Mr. Wenham, forms no obstacle to the ordinary use of the instrument, and the definition even of the highest powers with the binocular body is scarcely impaired. It consists of a small prism mounted in a brass box (Plate XX. fig. 3), which slides into an opening immediately above the object-glass (fig. 1, I), and reflects one half of the rays, which form an image of the object, into an additional tube (B) attached at an inclination to the ordinary body (C). One half of the rays take the usual course, with their conditions unaltered; and the remainder, although reflected twice, show no loss of light or definition worthy of notice, if the prism be well made.

As the eyes of different persons are not the same distance apart, the first and most important point to observe in using the "binocular" is, that each eye has a full and clear view of the object; this is easily tried by closing each eye alternately without moving the head, when it may be found that some adjustment is necessary by racking out the draw-tubes (D, E) by the milled head (K), which will increase the distance of the centres; or when moved in the contrary direction, they will suit those eyes that are nearer together.

If the prism be drawn back until stopped by its catch (fig. 3, F), the field of view in the inclined body is darkened, and the whole aperture of the object-glass passes into the main body as usual, neither the prism nor the additional body interfering in any way with the ordinary use of the microscope. By pressing back the spring-catch (fig. 3, F) of the prism, it can be withdrawn altogether for the purpose of being wiped; this should be done frequently and very carefully, *on all four surfaces*, with a perfectly clean cambric or silk handkerchief or a piece of wash-leather; but no hard substance must be used.

This construction of binocular body can be applied to any of the microscope-stands already described and drawn with the single body only. The first few plates of this work were engraved before Mr. Wenham's contrivance, or the illustrations would have included a binocular body in each instance, as it is now but seldom that we send out instruments with only the single body.

The most suitable kind of illumination for the binocular microscope has been already alluded to, and includes all those methods in which the light is thrown upon the upper surface; but for those objects that are semitransparent, as sections of bone or teeth, Diatomaceæ, living aquatic animalcules, &c., the dark-field illumination, by means of the parabolic reflector, will give a very good result. For the illumination of perfectly transparent objects, it is best to diffuse the light by placing various substances under the object, such as tissue-paper, ground glass, very thin porcelain, or a thin film of bees-wax run between two pieces of thin glass.

When employing the polarizing apparatus with the "binocular," the analyzer is fitted into an adapter (fig. 2), which applies immediately between the object-glass and the prism, with the means of revolving the prism by turning its tube round at opposite slots in the sides of the adapter, and the effects are exceedingly beautiful.

Although the binocular body makes the various features of an object so distinct and so easy to distinguish, yet the representation of them in drawings is extremely difficult, because the stereoscopic appearance can only be given by the management of the shadows: this has been attempted in the following illustrations:—cast skin of silkworm, Plate IX.; splinter of lucifer-match, Plate XI.; tarsus of spider and structure of feather, Plate XII.; *Arachnoidiscus Japonicus*, Plate XIII.; and Polycystina from Barbadoes earth, Plate XIV. To see these illustrations with the best result, they should be held so that the light falls on them from the top right-hand corner of the plate; only one eye should be used; and if the margin round the drawing be cut off by looking through the hand when nearly closed, the effect is considerably improved.

Sundry Apparatus.—Live-boxes and Trough.

To confine small living objects for examination under the microscope, different pieces of apparatus are used, according to the size or the nature of the object. Those that are dry and active may be secured in a live-box (Plate XXI. figs. 1 & 4). This consists of two parts: the lower piece (fig. 4, a) is a brass plate, with a short piece of tube (b) in the centre, carrying a circular piece of thick glass (c) at the top; over this fits the upper piece or cap (d), carrying a thin glass. The object is held by the pressure of the two glasses, and the amount of separation may be varied at pleasure by sliding the cap more or less on. The thin glass is in a cell, and may be changed or replaced by unscrewing the top milled ring (e).

A smaller live-box is shown in fig. 1.

These pieces of apparatus answer well for many objects in fluid; but if employed in this way, the quantity of water, or whatever it may be, should, if possible, be limited, as shown by the accompanying figure, in which the small central ring represents the appearance of a drop of water when held between the glasses of a live-box. The object, if small enough, may be confined thus, either with or without pressure, whereas, if the fluid be in excess, the objects will move about over too large a space, or frequently they reach the edge of the live-box and disappear altogether.

When fluid objects are very small and cannot be injured by moderate pressure, a very simple and efficient plan is to use the plate-slip (fig. 5, *a*); the fluid is placed upon this, and then covered with a thin piece of glass (*b*), which is prevented sliding off by the ledge (*d*).

The glass trough (figs. 2 & 3) is intended for larger objects in water; it must be used with its thinner plate of glass (fig. 3, *a*) in front. The modes of confining the objects, and keeping them near the front surface, must vary according to circumstances. For many it is a good plan to place the piece of glass (*b*) diagonally in the trough, its lower edge being kept in its place by a strip (*c*) at the bottom; then if the object introduced be heavier than water, it will sink till stopped by the sloping plate (*b*). Sometimes the whalebone-spring (*d*) may be applied behind this plate to advantage, with the wedge (*e*) in front to regulate the depth.

The glass tubes (fig. 6) are employed to catch any animalcule or other object that may be swimming about in a vessel of water.

If a finger be pressed close upon the small opening at the rounded end (*a*), the other end of the tube may be dipped in the water to any extent without the water entering the tube; but immediately the finger is lifted off, the water rushes up to the same level as that in the vessel, and together with it any animalcules which were near the lower and of the tube; the finger is placed again upon the small opening at the top of the tube, which can then be removed, together with its contents, from the vessel.

Compressors.

In many cases, objects require careful and yet considerable pressure whilst under the microscope, and there are many contrivances for the purpose.

Screw Live-box.

In the screw live-box (Plate XXI. figs. 9 & 10) the pressure is produced by two small spiral springs (a, a) acting against the upper plate (b), on the top surface of which a piece of thin glass is held by two springs (c, c); the lower plate holds a thick circular glass, and outside it is a milled ring (d), on which the upper plate is constantly pressed; the distance between the two glasses is regulated by the milled ring (d), which screws up or down, and two pins (e, e) prevent the plate turning round.

Lever Compressor.

The lever compressorium (figs. 13 & 14) has also a thick glass on the bottom plate; but the thin glass is cemented in a ring at the extremity of an arm or lever (a), which is moved up or down by turning the small screw (b). In this instrument the amount of pressure is the force imparted by the screw (b), and it is very considerable; it is equally distributed over the glasses by the ring (c) being swung in the centres (d, d), and by the semicircle (e) having a revolving fitting at (f); the lever (a) can be turned on one side, so as to expose both glasses when they want cleaning, or when the object is to be changed.

Wenham's Compressor.

Wenham's compressor (figs. 7 & 8) was designed especially for use with the parabolic reflector or achromatic condenser. The bottom plate (a) is very thin, and a circular thin glass is cemented in the middle; the top plate (b) is a thin brass arm, also carrying a circular thin glass cemented to it; the pressure is imparted by a spring or set which is given to the arm (b), and the two pieces of glass will approach or separate according to the direction in which the small milled head (c) is turned; the arm will also turn aside, as in the lever compressor. The simple construction of Wenham's compressor makes it a very easy and convenient instrument to use; it has, however, one or two disadvantages—the two pieces of glass do not move in parallel directions, and the amount of pressure is rather limited.

Reversible Compressors.

The next two compressors are our own contrivance, and both of them individually combine in one piece of apparatus the excellences of those already described, together with the following new qualities: viz., a parallel and equal compression, with an immediate action up or down; the means of turning the compressor over, so as to see both sides of an object without disturbing it; the use of thin glass only either at top or bottom; and lastly, such restrictions in the thickness of the brass-work as permit the use of the achromatic condenser, or the parabolic reflector, on either side of the object.

Mr. Slack suggested the basis of the construction in each case; he proposed that two oblong pieces of thin glass (fig. 15) should each be secured to a separate brass plate by the heads of two screws; spaces were then to be made for the heads of these screws in each opposing plate, and the two pieces of glass could be brought close together. This simple plan has great advantages: the pieces of glass are easily cut; for no great nicety of size is required, and they can be changed, or replaced, without difficulty and with little loss of time.

The "parallel plate compressor" (figs. 11 & 12) consists of two brass plates, furnished with thin glass, as already described, and connected by four small rods (a): this is in fact the commonest parallel-rule motion, and very nearly a vertical one; for when the plates are near together, the position of the connecting rods is such as to cause no perceptible end-movement. The brass plates, when about $\frac{1}{10}$th of an inch from each other, are kept apart by two springs, which supply the separating power, the compressing force being given by a small screw (b) with a conical end, attached to the one plate, working into a corresponding recess in the other plate; the first hold the point of the screw gets is at the bottom of the recess, so that the plates are drawn together as the screw advances. When the inner surfaces of the thin glasses want cleaning, or when the object or the glasses have to be changed, the screw (b) must be brought quite back, and the plates will then separate to the extent of a full inch.

In the "cell compressor" (figs. 16, 17, & 18), the thin glasses are secured to two circular plates of brass; the one fits the ring (fig. 18), and the other the counter ring (fig. 16) of a brass cell (fig. 17, a); when these are screwed together, the plates approach each other, or when unscrewed, they separate, and some slight intermediate brass springs counteract any loss of time that there may be in the screws or in the fittings of the circular plates. Two upright pins in a flat brass plate (fig. 17, *b*) pass through both the circular brass plates to prevent them turning round whilst the cell is screwed or unscrewed, and a small screw (*c*), working by a slight taper against a push-piece (*d*), holds the cell itself firmly in a sunken ring of the brass plate (*b*), into which it drops. For cleaning the glasses, &c., the circular plates may be entirely separated by unscrewing the cell. The chief novelty in both of these compressors is the opportunity they afford of examining both sides of an object whilst under pressure. The "parallel plate compressor" may be turned over altogether, and used from either side; in the "cell compressor," after the push-piece is loosened by slightly unscrewing the small milled head (*c*), the cell will lift out of the sunken ring and off the pins, to be placed on again with whichever side is wished uppermost.

Frog Plate.

The frog plate (fig. 19) supplies the means for viewing the circulation of the blood in the web of the frog's foot, and consists of a long thin brass plate (*a, a*), with a square aperture (*b*) at one end covered with a piece of glass. A small bag is supplied, in which the whole of the frog is put, except one hind leg; and to prevent this being drawn in, the neck of the bag should be pulled tight; the frog, thus confined, is then secured to the unglazed end of the brass plate by ribbon wound over it and through the holes at the sides of the plate, the ends being held by a spring underneath. The foot is next drawn out over the glass (*b*), and the web extended by fastening to the extremity of the toes, pieces of fine silk which can be wound round the pins (*c, c*). The glazed end of the plate must be clamped firmly to the stage of the microscope, and the frog as well as its foot should be constantly moistened with cold water; if also a piece of thin glass with water underneath be placed over the part of the web that is under examination, the effect is much improved.

Camera Lucida.

Wollaston's camera lucida, when applied to the achromatic microscope, is of the greatest use and importance; by its aid the most intricate structure of objects can be drawn with perfect accuracy and to an exact scale.

This piece of apparatus (Plate XXII. figs. 6, 7, & 8) slides on in the place of the cap of either eyepiece, with its flat side (fig. 7, *a*) uppermost, as shown also in fig. 8, which is a drawing to scale of the camera lucida when in use. The body of the microscope must be in a horizontal position, and a piece of paper laid upon the table should be exactly ten inches from the flat side of the prism. Then if the eye be placed so that its pupil is divided as it were by the edge of the prism (see accompanying figure, in which *a* represents the pupil of the eye and *b* the top surface of the prism), the object will appear 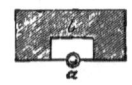 upon the paper, and can be traced on it by a pencil, the point of which will also be seen. Only one eye is to be used; and the light must be regulated so that no more than is really necessary is upon the object, whilst a full light is thrown upon the paper. Perfect steadiness of the eye is also necessary, and the eyebrow may be gently rested upon the prism-fitting as shown in fig. 8. Any one who cannot see to read distinctly at ten inches should use a lens in the position shown in figs. 6 & 8; it must be convex for long sight, and concave for short sight: in general the former only is supplied, but it is easily changed when necessary.

It must not be supposed that any carefully finished drawing can be made with the camera lucida; this is seldom possible; and when the object to be sketched is irregular on the surface, or larger than the field of view, it often requires no little care and patience to retain the relative position of the parts correctly; but considerable facility is soon acquired, and when observers who are quite unable to draw from the eye alone succeed in producing a faithful representation of an object, the result is most gratifying and frequently of some value, more especially if the specimen be not permanent. It is well known amongst observers that generally no minute comparison of objects can be made without drawings, and it is almost impossible to obtain such without the aid of the camera lucida; at the present time there are many illustrations of objects which are completely puzzling and comparatively worthless because they are not drawn to scale, but merely represent the appearances presented to the eye of the artist.

If there be substituted in the place of the object a piece of glass ruled into 100ths and 1000ths of an inch, termed a stage micrometer (fig. 3 or 4), its divisions can be marked on the same or another piece of paper, and by comparing them with the drawing of the object, the most accurate measurement can be made. The whole of Nobert's lines (Plate VIII.) and the markings on *Navicula rhomboides* (Plate VII. fig. 13) were measured in this way.

In Plate XXII. fig. 11 is a simple sketch to illustrate the usefulness and capabilities of the camera lucida; it represents the stellate tissue as occurring in the transverse section of a rush (*Juncus conglomeratus*), very commonly used in London for tying up bunches of watercresses. The left-hand portion of the sketch is the mere outline exactly as drawn by the aid of the camera lucida, the right-hand portion being touched up more or less to show how it may be finished if necessary, and at the bottom are traced 100ths and 1000ths of an inch to serve as a scale for measurement.

The magnifying power can be easily ascertained by comparing the magnified stage-micrometer lines traced by aid of the camera lucida with a rule divided into inches and tenths: thus, supposing $\frac{1}{100}$th of an inch, when marked on the paper, to measure 1 inch and $\frac{3}{10}$ths, the magnifying power would be 130; but in such calculations particular care must be taken that the distance from the edge of the camera lucida to the paper is exactly 10 inches, as this is the standard distance of distinct vision with the naked eye.

The Micrometers.

The following is a description by the late Mr. George Jackson, who was the inventor of this method of using micrometers with the compound microscope:—

"In ordinary observation, when no drawing is made, a micrometer in the eyepiece is the readiest method of measuring. But here it is obvious that we shall be comparing an *enlarged* image of the object with the divisions themselves, and not with *their enlarged image*. It is therefore necessary to ascertain the value of these divisions with each of the object-glasses of the microscope; or, in other words, to determine the relation which the micrometer in the eyepiece bears to the *image* of the one on the stage, subject to the same magnifying power that is to be applied to the object to be measured.

"Insert the proper micrometer (Plate XXII. fig. 2) in the eyepiece (see fig. 1), and adjust the upper lens (a) by its screw, so as to see the lines clearly when the light comes through the body of the instrument. Place a micrometer (fig. 3 or 4), divided into 100ths and 1000ths of an inch, on the stage, adjust the focus, and make the two sets of lines parallel by turning the eyepiece; then notice how many divisions in the latter correspond to one in the former. Suppose that nineteen and a half cover one-hundredth of an inch (fig. 5, *a*), by carefully adjusting the length of the draw-tube, the coincidence may be rendered exact at 20 divisions (fig. 5, *b*). Then, as twenty divisions cover one-hundredth of an inch, 2000 (20×100) will cover an inch, and each division will be equal to 1-2000th of an inch.

" In doing this with each object-glass, the draw-tube of the microscope should be so adjusted as to give a number that can be reduced to a decimal fraction by multiplying or dividing by a single figure; but if it be preferred to express the dimension by a simple vulgar fraction, we have merely to divide the number of divisions in an inch by the observed number. Thus, if the length of an object be eight divisions of the above scale (8-2000ths), it will be 1-250th of an inch, or decimally ·004.

" A memorandum should be made, in a tabular form, of the value of the eyepiece micrometer with each object-glass, together with the length of the tube drawn out, so that the instrument may be readjusted for measuring without repeating the above operation: thus—

"*Value of each division of Eyepiece Micrometer with the following Object-glasses.*

Object-glass.	Amount of tube drawn out, in tenths of an inch.	Fraction of an inch.	Decimal of an inch.
$\frac{2}{5}$	7	$\frac{1}{2000}$	·0005

" When moving the lines to their coincidence, the action of the stage will be found rather too quick; but the most correct adjustment can be made by the small screw (fig. 2, *a*) attached to the eyepiece micrometer."

Indicator.

Quekett's indicator (Plate XXII. figs. 9 & 10) is a fine pointer, fitted in the interior of the eyepiece, and capable of being turned in or out of the field of view by means of the small quadrant (fig. 9, *a*). It answers admirably for the very useful purpose of indicating some particular part of an object; and any of the eyepieces can be furnished with it.

Double Nosepiece.

Brooke's double nosepiece facilitates the change from one object-glass to another, and avoids the loss of time incurred by screwing and unscrewing in the ordinary way. This piece of apparatus (Plate XXII. fig. 14) is attached to the microscope by the screw-piece (*a*); two object-glasses are screwed to the extremities (*b, b*), and, by merely rotating the arm (*c, c*) on the centre (*d*), either object-glass may be brought into the position for use: a pin (*e*) in each instance forms a stop to ensure correct centering.

Quadruple Nosepiece.

We have extended the same principle as that of the foregoing to a quadruple nosepiece (Plate XXII. fig. 13); this is applied to the microscope by a screw-piece, as in the double one; but the object-glasses are changed in position by drawing the plate (fig. 13, *a*), to which they are screwed, a little forward, to release it from a pin, when it may be turned round, and a slight spring, confined in the top (*b*), will press the plate home again, when the next object-glass will be only central with the body of the microscope.

Leeson's Goniometer.

This instrument (Plate XXII. fig. 12) is admirably adapted for measuring the angles of microscopic crystals. It consists of a circular divided plate, above which a Biot's double-refracting prism is mounted so as to admit of rotation by means of the arm (A), which also serves as an index-hand. The whole piece of apparatus fits on the eyepiece, to the flange of which it is secured by a pin, which drops into a corresponding hole.

When a crystal, or any angle of a crystal, is viewed through the prism of the goniometer, there will appear two images, which may be made to occupy various relative positions by revolving the prism, as shown in the annexed woodcuts, figs. 1, 2, & 3.

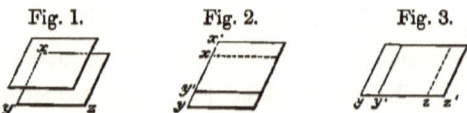

Fig. 1.   Fig. 2.   Fig. 3.

Let x, y, z be the angle to be measured: hold the arm (Plate XXII. fig. 12, A) at zero, and revolve the prism by the milled ring (B, B) until the lines forming one side of the angle to be measured coincide in both images, as, for instance, the lines x, y, x', y' (fig. 2), then move the arm over the graduated circle until the two lines forming the other side of the angle y, z, y', z' are made to coincide (fig. 3); the amount of rotation thus obtained is the measure of the angle, or its complement, according to the direction in which the arm is moved. Instead of starting from zero, it is of course sufficient to take the difference of the readings in the two positions.

Maltwood's Finder.

A "finder," as applied to the microscope, is the means of registering the position of any particular object in a slide, so that it may be referred to at a future time, and by any microscopist who possesses the finder.

The subject of the best form was very fully discussed in the pages of the 'Quarterly Journal of Microscopical Science;' amongst the various schemes we selected the following, which was proposed by Mr. Maltwood, and it has now become a universal standard of reference.

It consists of a glass slide, $3 \times 1\frac{1}{4}$ inches, with a scale (a)

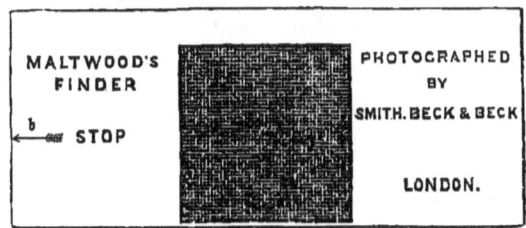

True size.

occupying one square inch, and consisting of 2500 squares, each of which is separately numbered with a longitude and latitude.

The scale is in each instance at an exact distance from the bottom and left-hand end of the glass slide, which, when in use, should rest upon the ledge of the stage of the microscope, and be pushed against a stop at the end; this stop, which is best as a simple pin, should be about one inch and a half from the centre of the stage, and at a point from the ledge indicated by an arrow upon the finder at b.

The object-slide must be placed under the microscope with the same care as the finder; and when the particular object is in the field of view, remove the object-slide, put the finder in its place, and read the numbers of the square that comes into view; this may be recorded upon the object-slide; and to refer to the same object at a future time, the process has only to be reversed, by first finding the particular square of the finder, and then by placing the object-slide in its place.

There is an easy way of recording the numbers by which each square may be subdivided into 5; thus:—Supposing the following figure to represent one of the squares; if the object should be out of the centre of the square, put two lines in addition to the figures, to indicate the particular corner in which it occurs; thus, if it is a, write $\overline{\left|\dfrac{24}{12}\right.}$, if at b, $\overline{\left.\dfrac{24}{12}\right|}$, if at c, $\underline{\left|\dfrac{24}{12}\right.}$, or if at d, $\underline{\left.\dfrac{24}{12}\right|}$, whilst if near the centre, the figures $\dfrac{24}{12}$ may be recorded without any lines.

We have taken great care to preserve an exact uniformity in the size of the scale and in its position on the slide, so that the registrations may avail any microscopist who possesses one of these finders; we should at the same time mention that the ledges on the stages of microscopes are generally made at an angle, and when this angle varies it may make a slight difference in the readings from the finder; and, principally on this account, we have adhered to Mr. Maltwood's original size of fiftieths of an inch, rather than any smaller size, for the squares in the scale.

Microscope-Lamps.

One of the greatest advantages possessed by the microscope is its entire fitness for use at night; but to experience the full enjoyment of it at this time, the illumination must be suitably arranged and sufficiently bright; any of the four lamps shown in Plate XXIII. are suited for the purpose. Fig. 1 is known as the " Cambridge reading-lamp," and burns oil. Figs. 2 & 3 are for Belmontine, Leucoline, or some other of those kinds of oil, which are admirably adapted for the purpose, if they are only properly selected and prepared; we are now in treaty for some specially made for use with the microscope, which we expect to be most brilliant, perfectly safe, and free from any unpleasant smell. Fig. 4 is a gas-lamp with a flexible tube for a connexion. All these lamps are provided with the means of raising and lowering the light upon the stems (A), and also with movable shades (B) for protecting the eyes from any annoying glare. The intensity of the light may also be increased or diminished by appliances common to other lamps, and therefore not requiring explanation here. In any case when a wick is used, it should be carefully dried before being put into the lamp; and if there be any hardening or incrustation at the top of the wick after it has been used, it should be cut or rubbed off previous to being lighted. But above all give the glass chimney a wipe each time before it is put on; there is no need to clean it all the way up, but any smear or fog below the top of the flame forms a serious obstruction to good illumination.

Microscope-Table.

However absorbing and sometimes exclusive microscopical observations may be, there are many occasions upon which the cooperation of other observers is required, and not unfrequently the microscope is enlisted in the sociable entertainments of an evening. Under either of these circumstances a frequent change of seat, or even, if the instrument be placed perpendicularly, the constant standing, detracts much from any pleasure, and makes a quiet study unnecessarily irksome and disturbing.

The table (Plate XXIII. fig. 5) is contrived to obviate these annoyances; it will comfortably accommodate three people sitting, and by revolving the top, the microscope may be passed round without any one rising: this principle can be, and frequently is, extended to tables of much larger size, but the arrangement here shown is the one more generally approved.

Firmness of construction is most essential in these tables, and the revolving fitting especially has to be made with great care. The manufacture throughout is of the best description, consequently their cost contrasts rather unfavourably with that of much of the furniture of the present day; but tables of inferior construction have only proved most annoying, or entirely useless, when required for microscopical purposes.

Another convenient and simple method of passing the microscope to any number of persons seated at an ordinary table without disturbing the adjustments of the instrument, is shown in Plate XXVII. fig. 2. It consists of a neatly framed wooden stand, covered with leather on the top, which is sufficiently large to receive the microscope and lamp; and the under side is provided with four carefully made brass casters, so that the stand and all that is upon it may be pushed about smoothly in any direction that may be required.

Cases for Microscopes.—First-class.

The microscope-stands, the apparatus, and the object-glasses are almost invariably packed in some kind of case; it is a subject we have paid considerable attention to, because upon it the good preservation of a microscope, whether at home or when travelling, very much depends.

Plate XXV. shows a best Spanish mahogany case, containing a large best binocular microscope complete; the tripod of the stand is fitted on a board (A) at the bottom of

CASES FOR MICROSCOPES. 71

the case, which confines the instrument to a certain position, and much facilitates the sliding of it in or out; at the top, the eyepiece-caps slide in two grooves, and a removable block (D) in the left-hand one fills up a vacant space between the front of the eyepiece and the door. Two boxes (E & F), containing the apparatus, slide in at the sides of the instrument, and are secure in their places when the case is closed. The bull's-eye condenser packs on some blocks (G & H) at the back, and the draw-tube slides into two holes on the left at I; with these two exceptions, the whole of the apparatus and object-glasses fit into the various holes or recesses cut in the boards placed in the insides of the two boxes as shown in Plate XXVI.; various blocks, faced with velvet, are fastened to the lids of the boxes, so that when closed and secured by the hooks, the whole of the apparatus will remain undisturbed, even when turned upside-down or shaken. When there is a smaller quantity of apparatus than that shown in Plate XXV., only one box is used. We also make a cheaper form of outside case in Honduras mahogany.

Our large best binocular microscope, complete in every respect, may be made exceedingly portable by using a folding tripod stand and a movable stage; with these alterations the whole will pack in a case, the outside measure of which is only 19 inches long, $9\frac{1}{4}$ inches broad, and 5 inches deep.

Second-class Cases.

The second-class instruments are packed with the same care as those of the first class, but generally in flat cases, such as the one represented in Plate XXVII. The microscope is shown with but little apparatus; there is, however, abundant room in the case for any additions; we also specify in our catalogue for upright cases of this class.

Another plan which may be adopted for keeping any microscope at home is a simple bell-glass placed over a base, to which the stand of the instrument is fitted; but this method is almost invariably additional to the ordinary arrangement previously described.

THE THIRD-CLASS MICROSCOPES.

THESE instruments are intended to meet a want that has been much felt by students and others, who have been desirous of possessing an instrument equal to their requirements, whether in physiology, chemistry, or the minute forms of animal or vegetable life, but have not been able or not disposed to incur the cost of such as are larger or more elaborate.

Of this class we give descriptions of two different forms of Stand, distinguished from each other by the titles of the Popular and the Educational Microscopes.

THE POPULAR MICROSCOPE.

This entirely new form of Stand has been contrived because the construction of the Educational Instrument, described at p. 89, was not suited to the addition of Wenham's Binocular Body. Whilst, therefore, the optical arrangement of the Popular Microscope remains exactly the same as that of the Educational, the stand is greatly improved, without any additional cost.

The object-glasses and eyepieces of the Popular Microscope are so similar in appearance to the best ones figured in Plate V., that any additional illustrations would only appear superfluous; but the magnifying powers and other

74   THE POPULAR OBJECT-GLASSES.

particulars more especially relating to the object-glasses of this microscope are given in the following list.

The Popular Series of Achromatic Object-glasses.

The object-glasses in the following list are intended for all kinds of general use in which any very large aperture is not necessary.

There are many persons who would not, with ordinary objects, and using only the first and second eyepieces, see any difference between these powers and the very best, the corrections being perfect, and the workmanship really good so far as the aperture goes.

With severe test-objects, and employing the third or higher eyepieces, the difference is very perceptible; but many who work with the microscope never require this high-class performance; and the price of these object-glasses is very considerably below that of the best.

Focal length.		Linear magnifying power, nearly, with eyepieces		Degrees of angle of aperture.
		No. 1.	No. 2.	
	Draw-tubes			
2 inches	closed	24	40	10
1½ inch	ditto	29	48	15
1 inch	ditto	55	90	22
½ inch	ditto	120	200	40
¼ inch	ditto	210	350	75
⅛ inch	ditto	420	700	85

All these object-glasses have the Universal Screw (see p. 6).

With the ½-inch and higher powers the condition of the chromatic and spherical aberrations may be considerably altered by the use of different thicknesses of thin glass, or other media, in covering the object.. As a provision to compensate for the errors arising from such causes, the front tube of each of these object-glasses is made to slide for a very short distance; and when pulled out as far as it will go, the object-glass is adjusted for an uncovered object, and the tube must be pushed back more or less for an object that is covered, the extreme adjustment being for glass ·01 thick.

Description of the Stand.

The construction of the Popular Microscope (see figs. 11, 12, and 13) is as follows:—

The body, A (in these illustrations shown as binocular), is carried by a strong arm, B; and this is attached to a square bar, C, which may be moved up or down by a rackwork and pinion in the lower part of the stand, where the stage, D, and the mirror, E, are attached.

The base, F, is triangular; and it is connected with the parts of the instrument already described by a broad stay, G, which moves on centres at the top and bottom, so as to allow the end of the tube, H, to fit by its projecting pin into various holes along the medial line of the base. With this arrangement, if the body of the microscope be required in a more or less inclined position (see fig. 11), four holes are provided near the extremity of the base for the pin of the tube to fit into. A hole near the stout pin, L, is used when a vertical position is wanted (see fig. 12); while to obtain the horizontal position, shown in fig. 13, the pin of the tube is placed in a hole in the stud, K, the inner surface of the stay, G, resting at the same time on the top of the stout pin, L. This form of construction is entirely new, and has the following advantages:—it is strong, firm, and yet light; the instrument cannot alter from any particular inclination it is put into, which is not unfrequently the case when the ordinary joint works loose; and in every position the heavier part of the stand is brought over the centre of the base to ensure an equality of balance.

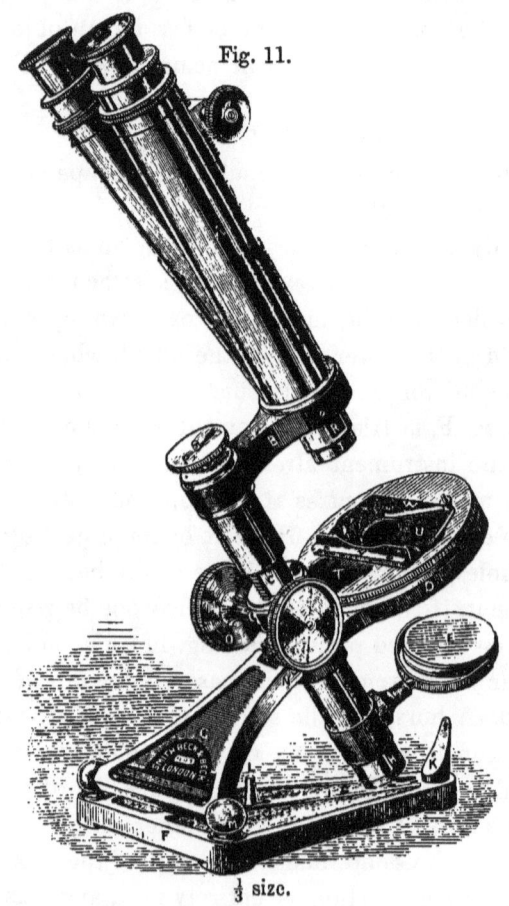

Fig. 11.

⅓ size.

Directions for Use.

To adjust the focus of the object-glass, turn the milled

head, O, for a quick movement, or the milled head, P, for a slow one.

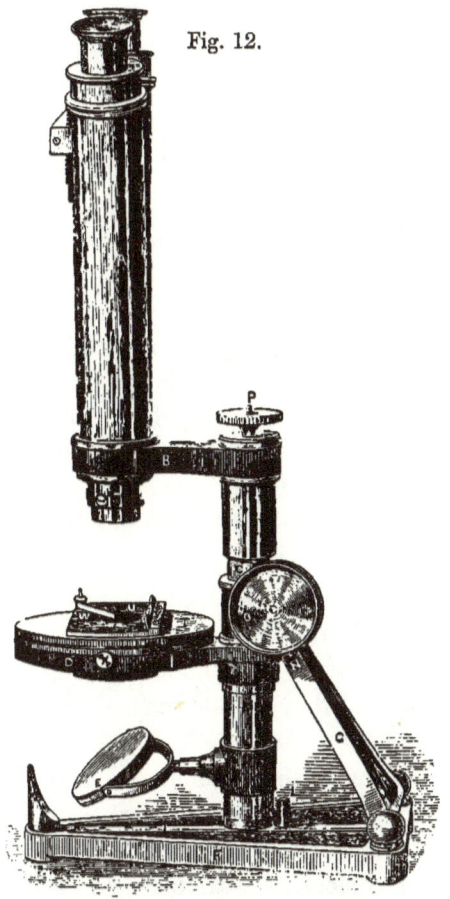

Fig. 12.

⅓ size.

The stage, D, is circular; and upon it fits a plate, T; this again carries the object-holder, U, which is provided with a ledge, V, and a light spring, W; it is held on the plate T by a spring underneath, so that it can be moved about easily and smoothly by one or by both hands. The small spring,

W, is fastened to the object-holder by a milled head, which will unscrew; so that the position of the spring may be altered to give more or less pressure upon the edge of the object, or it may be removed altogether, if necessary.

When a stage with only a flat surface is required, the object-holder, U, may be removed by unscrewing, from the under side of the plate, T, two small milled heads which connect a circular spring with the object-holder; or, by removing the plain stage altogether, an extra simple flat plate may be substituted.

Beneath the stage there is a cylindrical fitting for the reception of a diaphragm, or for any additional apparatus that may be required in that position.

The mirror, E, besides swinging in a rotating semicircle, will slide up or down the tube, H, or it will turn on either side for oblique illumination.

The *light* should in general be on the left of the observer; the best is that from a white cloud on a bright day; but a satisfactory effect can be obtained from a wax or Palmer's candle, if protected by a glass, a Cambridge or Moderator oil-lamp, a small Paraffin or Belmontine lamp, or an Argand gas-burner, provided they are not more than 10 or 12 inches from the instrument.

The management of the illumination demands particular attention; that of a *transparent object* is produced by reflexion from the mirror below, which should most frequently have its centre coincident with the axis of the body, and should be at such a distance that the light reflected from it may nearly converge to a focus at the object: this distance will be about $2\frac{1}{2}$ inches when daylight is used; but the rays from a lamp or candle 10 or 12 inches from the mirror are so divergent, that the focus for them will be lengthened to about 3 inches; and the mirror may have to be slid up or down accordingly.

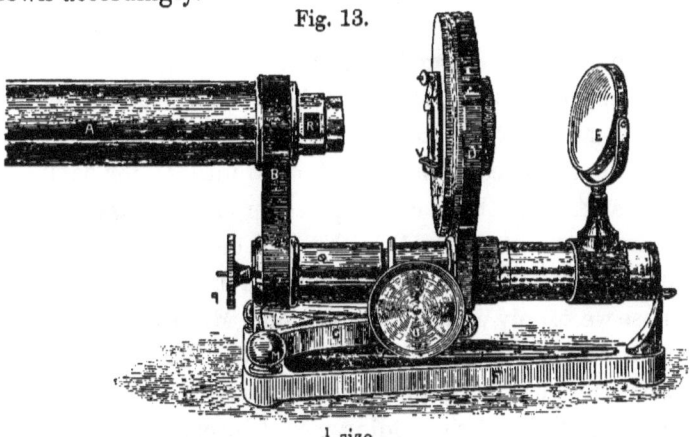

Fig. 13.

⅓ size.

Accurate adjustment of this focus is often required with the ¼-inch object-glass; and some details of objects, such as delicate striæ, are best seen with this glass when a strong light is thrown on them *obliquely* by turning the mirror on one side of the axis. With the 1-inch object-glass the light is generally in excess, and has to be lessened by fitting the *Diaphragm* (fig. 14) under the stage; this admits only so much light as passes through one or other of the two apertures in a small revolving disk, by which contrivance, together with sliding the diaphragm up more or less under the stage, every necessary variation can be made. The diaphragm is generally left in its place when the in-

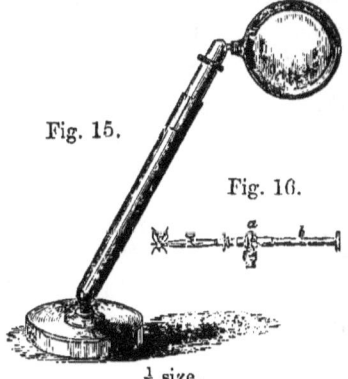

Fig. 14.

Fig. 15.

Fig. 16.

⅓ size.

strument is packed away; or, if there be a vacant space, it may be put in the *Tray* (fig. 20).

To illuminate opaque objects the light is thrown upon them from above; a *Small Condensing Lens* (fig. 15) mounted upon a separate stand, and capable of being turned in any direction, answers well for this purpose: its focus, for a lamp or candle 4 inches from it, is about 3 inches; for daylight, 2 inches. A large object can be placed upon the stage at once; but small ones are generally either laid on a piece of glass or held in the *Forceps* (fig.16): these are of a superior construction to those we supply with our Educational Microscope; they fit upon the pin at the top of the small milled head, which fastens the spring on the stage, and by the ball-and-socket movement at *a*, and the sliding wire *b*, every requisite movement can be obtained. In illuminating objects from above, all light that could enter the object-glass from below should be excluded; and the *Diaphragm* (fig. 14) will do this very effectually when placed under the stage, with the blank space of its revolving disk turned over the aperture.

A *Glass Plate* with a ledge, and some pieces of *Thin Glass* (fig. 17) are applicable for many purposes, but are specially intended for objects in fluid. Thus, a drop is placed upon the plate and covered by a piece of thin glass; or, the object being put upon the plate, and the thin glass over it, the fluid is applied near one side, and runs under by capillary attraction.

Fig. 17.

A pair of *Brass Pliers* (fig. 18) completes the necessary apparatus furnished with the microscope, and is kept, with the forceps and glass plate, in the space on the left-hand side of the *Tray*, fig. 19.

Fig. 18.

The *Case* is made of mahogany, French-polished, with brass hooks, a good lock, and a strong handle. To pack away the stand, it must first be put in the horizontal position (fig. 13); but no part has to be taken to pieces. At the right-hand end of the case, provision is made for all the apparatus. In the first place, a *Removable Tray* (fig. 19), lying at the bottom

Fig. 19.

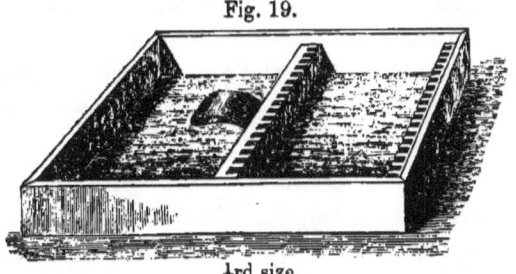

⅓rd size.

of the case, is divided into two spaces: the one is for keeping the forceps, pliers, glass plate, &c.; and the other is racked for 18 objects. Above this fits another *Tray* (fig. 20), which is

Fig. 20.

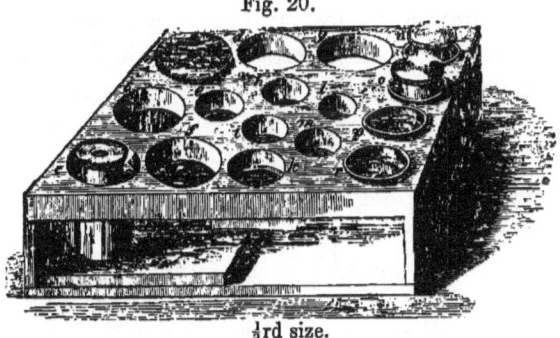

⅓rd size.

contrived to receive not only the object-glasses and apparatus already alluded to, and here shown in their places, but also the whole of the apparatus hereafter described. a is the diaphragm; c, the 2nd eyepiece; and n and o, the object-glasses, for which some brass cells are fitted in the board;

G

and when the object-glasses are put away, the engraved brass caps should always be screwed on, to prevent any dust settling on the inner glasses, which cannot be easily wiped.

The other spaces in the tray are arranged as follows:—in the holes, *a*, *b*, *d*, *g*, the achromatic condenser, the parabolic reflector, the dark-well holder, or the large polarizing prism will fit; the small analyzing prism will pack in *c*; the camera lucida in *k*; *p* and *r* are spaces for additional object-glasses; *l* and *m* will receive the 1-in. and ½-in. Lieberkuhns; an extra eyepiece can be packed at *f*; and *h* and *i* are finger- and thumb-holes for taking hold of the tray.

The whole or any part of the extra apparatus for which spaces are left in the *Tray*, and which is described in pages 83 to 88, may be added to the instrument at any time, without its being sent back to the makers.

Glass of any kind requires occasional cleaning; a piece of soft wash-leather is the best for the purpose.

The fronts of the *Object-glasses* may be carefully wiped; but if anything more be required, it must be done by the makers.

When cleaning the *Eyepieces*, which should be done *frequently*, the cells containing the glasses must be unscrewed and replaced one at a time, so that they may not be mixed.

Any dirt upon the *Eyepieces* may be detected by turning them round whilst looking through the instrument; but if the *Object-glasses* are not clean, or are injured, it will for the most part only be seen by the object appearing misty.

Wenham's Binocular Body.

Thus far in this description the Popular Microscope has been considered as having a single body only; the addition, therefore, of the Binocular Body, as shown in the illustrations, requires a few explanations and directions for use, which will be found in pp. 48 to 55, where there is a full description of the contrivance, in every way applicable to this instrument, excepting a slight difference in the fitting of the prism, which in the Popular Microscope can only be removed after a smaller milled head (fig. 12, S) has been unscrewed.

Mechanical Stage.

When the movement of the object requires greater nicety than a direct action from the hand can give, the plain stage may be taken off and replaced by *a Stage with Mechanical Movements* (fig. 21). By this arrangement the plate (*a*) with a fitting, sliding up or down, will receive the object, which can also be moved sideways, these two movements forming a quick adjustment; the slower movements in rectangular directions being given by turning the milled heads *b* and *c*, which, for convenience in use, are placed on the same spindle. For rotation of the object, the whole stage may be turned upon the bottom stage-plate, which is central with the body; and consequently the part of the object that is under examination will always remain in the field of view during the rotation.

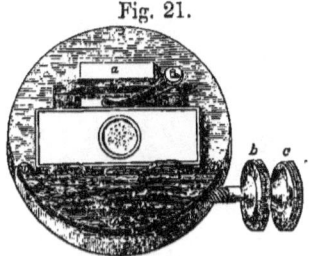

Fig. 21.

⅓rd size.

Additional Apparatus.

When the light from the concave mirror proves insufficient for any object requiring an intense transmitted light, the *Achromatic Condenser* (fig. 22) may be employed with advantage: this slides, by its tube, into the fitting under the stage of the instrument, in which it has to be moved up or down until the focus of its lenses falls upon the object, the light having been previously reflected in the proper direction by the flat mirror.

Fig. 22.   Fig. 23.   Fig. 24.

⅓rd size.

The *Illumination of Opaque Objects*, already described, must be more or less one-sided; and in most cases it is desirable that it should be so. An illumination on any or every side is, however, easily obtained, provided the object is not too large, by means of the *Lieberkuhn* (fig. 23). This is a silvered cup, which slides upon the front of the object-glass, and light thrown upwards by the mirror will be reflected by it down upon the object; it will then be found that, by slightly varying the inclination of the mirror, every necessary alteration in the direction of the illumination can be obtained. The *Lieberkuhn* here shown is intended for the 1-inch object-glass.

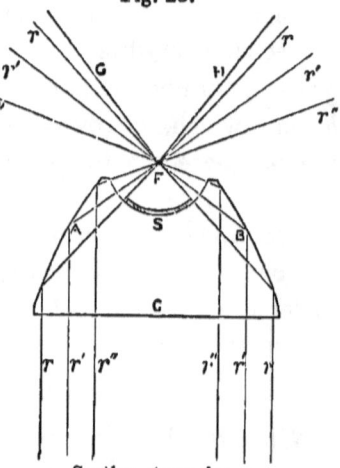

Fig. 25.

Section, true size.

It is in most cases necessary, when using the Lieberkuhn, to slide a *Dark Well* (fig. 24) under the stage, to prevent any light entering the object-glass direct from the mirror.

Dark-Field Illumination is, to appearance, a means of seeing a transparent object as an opaque one. The principle, however, is that all the light shall be thrown under the object, but so obliquely that it cannot enter the object-glass unless interrupted by the object: this is best accomplished by *Wenham's Parabolic Reflector* (fig. 26). It may be easily understood by reference to fig. 25, which represents it in section A B C, and shows that the rays of light, *r r' r''*, entering perpendicularly at its surface C, and then reflected by its parabolic surface A B to a focus at F, can form no part of the largest pencil of light admitted by the object-glasses and represented by G F H ; but an object placed at F will interrupt the rays and be strongly illuminated. A stop at S prevents any light from passing through direct from the mirror.

Fig. 26.

⅓rd size.

In this microscope, the *Parabolic Reflector* fits under the stage by the tube A (fig. 26), and the adjustment of its focus upon the object (which is when its apex almost touches it) is made by giving it a spiral motion when fitted in—that is, carefully pushing it up or down at the same time that it is turned round by the milled edge, B B. As the rays of light must be parallel when they enter it, a *Flat Mirror*, which in this case should be added to the instrument, is generally used; daylight will then require only direct reflexion, but the rays from an artificial source will have to be made parallel by putting the condenser (fig. 15) between the light and the mirror, about 1¾ inch from the former and 4½ inches from the latter. Nearly the whole surface of the mirror should be equally illuminated, which may be tested by temporarily placing upon it a card or piece of white paper. Parallel rays can also be obtained from the *Concave Mirror*, if the light is put about 2½ inches from it.

Polarized Light, invaluable to some microscopists, and to others a beautiful appliance by which many objects otherwise almost invisible are shown in every imaginable colour,

can here only be treated of by describing the way in which it is applied to this microscope by the following apparatus:—
A Nicol's prism as a Polarizer (A, fig. 27) fits, and can be turned round, under the stage; another prism, B, slides in the place of the cap of either eyepiece, and also revolves; or by unscrewing its outer tube, *c*, and its cap, *d*, it screws, as *e*, in the place of the back-stop, *f*, of either object-glass, and then the object-glass together with the prism are attached to the nosepiece of the microscope by the adapter (H), which has a revolving fitting at *k*. When the prism B is over the No. 2 eyepiece, the field of view is considerably cut off; and although it is not so when the prism is screwed above the object-glass, yet the definition is then somewhat impaired: its position therefore must be regulated by the character of the object. When only alternate black and white images are given by the prisms alone, a plate of selenite, G, will produce coloured ones.

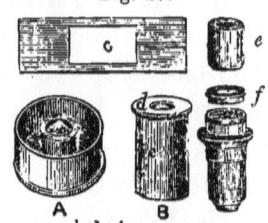

Fig. 27.

⅓rd size.

To draw an object, the *Camera Lucida* (fig. 28) is used. It slides on in the place of the cap of either eyepiece, with its flat side uppermost, as shown. The body of the microscope must be in a horizontal position, and the whole instrument has to be raised until the edge of the prism is exactly 10 inches from a piece of paper placed upon the table. If the side of the case be used for this purpose, the proper distance is exceeded by ¾ of an inch; but the paper may easily be raised this amount by some pad. The light must be so regulated that no more than is really necessary is upon the object, whilst a full light should be thrown upon the paper. Only one eye is to be used; and if one half of the pupil be directed over the edge of the prism, the object will appear upon the paper, and can be traced on it by a pencil, the point of which will also be seen. Should any blueness be visible in the field, the prism is pushed too far on, and should be drawn back till the colour disappears.

Fig. 28.

⅓rd size.

Substituting in the place of the object a piece of glass ruled into 1-100ths and 1-1000ths of an inch, termed a *Micrometer* (fig. 29), its divisions can be marked on the same or another piece of paper, and, by comparing them with the sketch, the object can be most accurately measured. These divisions also, if compared with a rule divided into inches and tenths, will give the magnifying power: thus, supposing 1-100th of an inch when marked on the paper measured 1 inch and $\frac{3}{10}$ths, the magnifying power would be 130.

The *Live-box* (fig. 30) hardly needs description: the object is confined between the glass, a, of the lower part, B, and that of the cap, C; the distance between them can be varied by sliding the latter more or less on. As the thin glass is only dropped into a slight recess in the top of the cap, and is held there by the heads of the two screws, it can be easily taken out for wiping, or be replaced by another when broken.

The *Glass Trough* (fig. 31), for larger objects in water, must be used with its thinner plate of glass, b, in front. The modes of confining such objects, and keeping them near

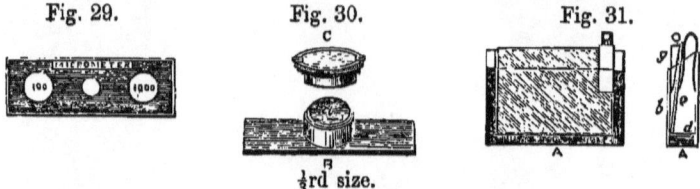

Fig. 29.   Fig. 30.   Fig. 31.

⅓rd size.

the front surface, must vary according to the occasion. For many it is a good plan to place a piece of glass, e, diagonally in the trough, its lower edge being kept in its place by a strip (d) at the bottom; then if the object introduced is heavier than water, it will sink till stopped by the sloping plate. Sometimes a very slight spring (f) may be applied behind this plate to advantage, with a wedge (g) in front to regulate the depth.

Arrangements are made for all those parts which may require cleaning. Thus, the Parabolic Reflector unscrews from the tube; the Nicol's Prisms will push out of their fittings; and the Camera-lucida Prism can be taken out by turning aside the plate that covers it.

THE EDUCATIONAL MICROSCOPE.

This is the first third-class instrument that we constructed; and although we consider the stand to be superseded by the Popular Microscope, last described, there are many persons who, not requiring a binocular body, are of opinion that the Educational Microscope possesses many advantages in its form and arrangement; we therefore give the following full description of the instrument.

Fig. 32.

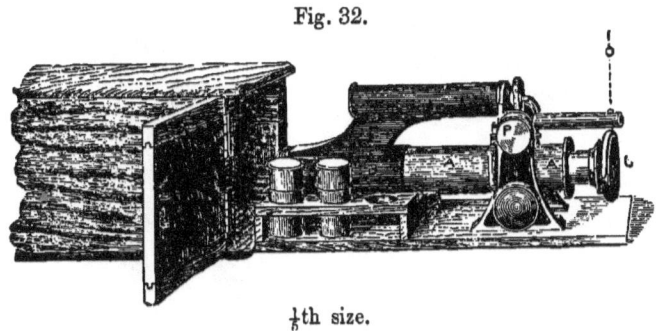

¼th size.

When the microscope is taken out of the case, as shown in fig. 32, first turn up the mirror G to O, and draw out the body, A; the stand, turning on the centre P, can then be placed in a perpendicular, horizontal, or any intermediate position. Next restore the mirror to its former place, slide the body, A, into the upper end of the tube B, and the instrument is ready for use. (See fig. 33.)

To adjust *the focus* of the Object-glass:—*A quick motion* is obtained by sliding the body, A, in the tube B; and *a slow motion* by turning the milled head, C. The *Stage*, D, has two springs, E, the pins of which may be inserted in any of the four holes, F, and by their pressure, which can be varied by pushing them more or less down, they will hold the ob-

90   THE EDUCATIONAL MICROSCOPE.

ject under them, or allow it to be moved about with the greatest nicety.

The *Mirror*, G, besides swinging in the rotating semicircle,

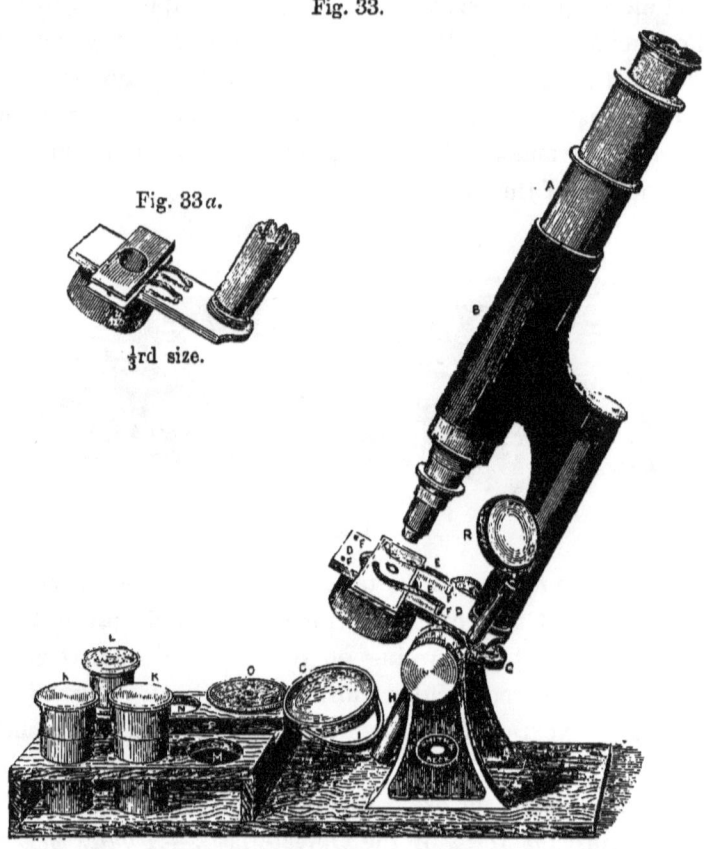

Fig. 33.

Fig. 33 a.

⅓rd size.

⅓rd size.

I, is on the tube H, which may be drawn down, or turned on either side.

There are some cases in which a supplementary stage

(fig. 33 a) may be found useful, as it entirely prevents the springs of the stage, E E (fig. 33), interfering with an object or its covering when under the microscope; such a stage can be used under all circumstances, except with the dark field and Lieberkuhn illuminations.

When the instrument is put away, the object-glasses are kept in the boxes, K. The eyepiece No. 1 is left in the body, and No. 2 fits in the space at L. The two vacant spaces in the board at M and N are for an additional object-glass, and a Lieberkuhn to be used with the 1-inch, if these should be required.

The diaphragm which fits under the stage is shown in fig. 34; this admits only so much light as will pass through its aperture (A), but by sliding it up more or less in the fitting, every necessary variation can be made, or the diaphragm may be used to exclude all light from below, in which case the small shutter, B, is turned over the aperture. The diaphragm packs in the board at O (fig. 33).

Fig. 34.

A small condensing lens, R, attached to one of the uprights of the stand answers well for the illumination of opaque objects: its focus for a lamp or candle four inches from it is about three inches; for daylight, $1\frac{3}{4}$ inch.

Fig. 35 shows the forceps which are supplied with the Educational Microscope, and the different ways in which they will hold small opaque objects.

Fig. 35.

The remaining apparatus, together with the object-glasses and eyepieces suitable for application to this stand, are the same as those already described under the Popular Microscope (pp. 83 to 88); but there is some difference in the way

92   THE EDUCATIONAL MICROSCOPE.

in which the extra apparatus is packed, as shown by the accompanying figure, which represents a small mahogany board provided with the various packings, and fitting into a groove near the top of the case.

Fig. 36.

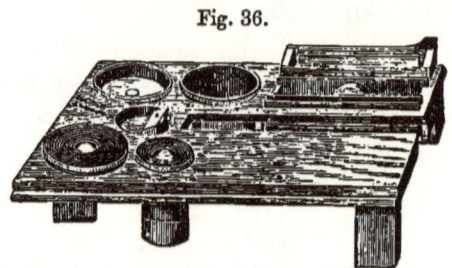

FOURTH CLASS.

THE UNIVERSAL MICROSCOPE.

This instrument is the result of an endeavour to make a very low-priced Compound Achromatic Microscope by reducing its construction to the simplest possible form, still retaining all that a really useful instrument requires, together with such an arrangement as would admit of considerable additions being made without returning the stand to the makers. These features, together with other details, are fully explained in the following description:—

The foundation of the stand is a large circular base (fig. 37, A), and near its circumference, on the left-hand side, is a strong pillar (B); at its top is the axis upon which the remainder of the instrument turns, and with so equal a balance as never to require more than a slight screwing down of the small milled head, C, to secure any particular position.

On the same centre as the axis is a large milled head, D, by turning which a quick motion is given to the body, E; and depending from the smaller part of the same milled head is a lever, F; this of itself hangs free, but when held at the lower end, and pressed sideways, either nearer or further from the pillar, it obtains a gripe upon the milled head, which can then be turned so slowly as to constitute a very good slow motion.

The quick-motion milled head and the slow-motion lever are always in the same position, and do not alter with any inclination of the body; they are also so low down, that in using them the hands are very little raised from the table;

THE UNIVERSAL MICROSCOPE.

Fig. 37.

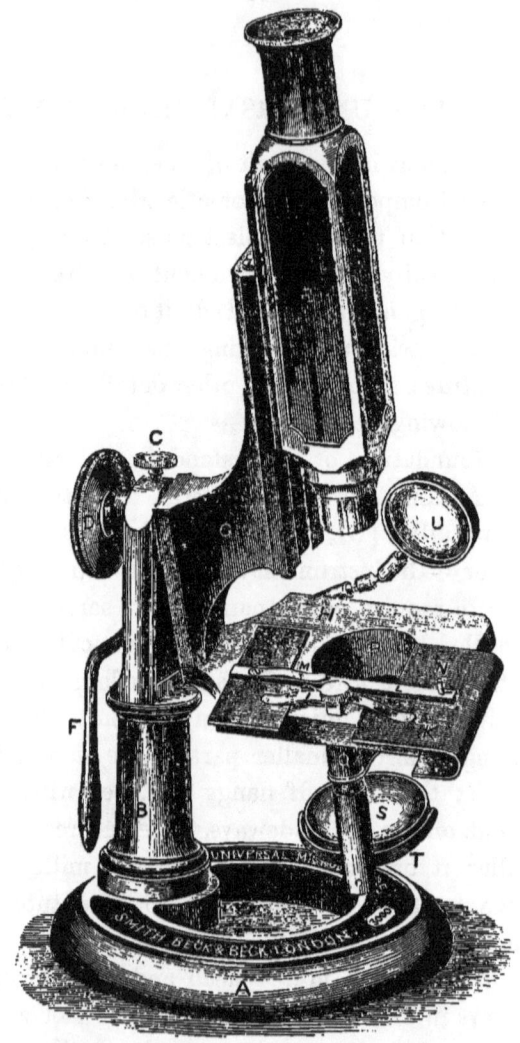

This illustration is drawn to a scale of half size.

this latter advantage also applies to the stage (H), which is screwed on at the lower end of the limb (G) at less than four inches from the bottom of the stand.

On the top of the stage is a double spring (I) branching right and left over a brass plate (K); on this there is a ledge (L) for the object to rest upon, and in continuation on the right-hand side the plate is bent over so that it may be firmly grasped by the fore and middle fingers underneath, and by the thumb above. With this arrangement the object can be moved freely in every direction, and will retain its position after the hand is withdrawn. If necessary, the short spring (M) may be used when the object has to be held firmly on the plate. The pin (N) is for holding the forceps. Beneath the stage is a cylindrical fitting (P) for all the apparatus required in that position.

Fig. 38.

The diaphragm (fig. 38) is, however, made a fixture to the mirror-stem; but it will turn away entirely on the left side, when necessary; it is provided with one small aperture (X) for the lower powers, and this can be closed by a small shutter (Y).

½ size.

A concave mirror (fig. 37, S) swings in a rotary semicircle (T) which is attached to an outside sliding tube, the inner tube being screwed beneath the stage; on the opposite side a condenser (U) is fixed for the illumination of opaque objects; it is provided with ball-and-socket joints, which afford any necessary movement, and also the means of turning it out of the way when not in use. Its focus for a lamp or candle five inches from it is about $2\frac{1}{2}$ inches; for daylight, $1\frac{3}{4}$ inch.

There are five object-glasses with which the Universal Microscope may be furnished, viz. 2-inch, 1-inch, ½-inch,

$\frac{1}{4}$-inch, and $\frac{1}{8}$-inch (fig. 39); they differ from the powers of all other instruments in having, a smaller-size screw for their attachment to the body, and the settings of their lenses made as short as possible, these variations having been made to suit them to the "Combined" and "Binocular" bodies, described further on.

Fig. 39.

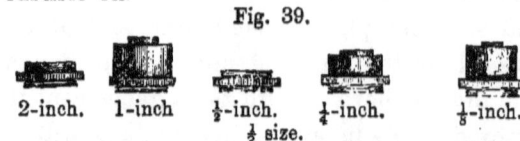

2-inch.   1-inch. $\frac{1}{2}$-inch. $\frac{1}{4}$-inch. $\frac{1}{8}$-inch.
$\frac{1}{2}$ size.

The eyepieces (fig. 40) are of a construction introduced by Kellner, and they give a flat and, for their size, a large field of view. Their chief fault will, we believe, prove a general advantage: any dust or moisture upon the field-lens is so annoyingly apparent from its being in the focus of the eye-lens, that those who use this form will be compelled to wipe the lenses frequently; and not only this, but they will soon learn the necessity for the constant examination and the occasional cleaning of every surface of glass that they have about their microscopes.

Fig. 40.

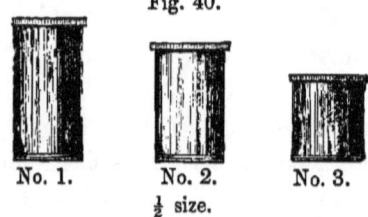

No. 1.   No. 2.   No. 3.
$\frac{1}{2}$ size.

The apertures of the object-glasses of the Universal Microscope and their linear magnifying powers when combined with the eyepieces are given in the following list, together with the increase that may be obtained by the addition of a lengthening tube to the body—an arrangement which, under many circumstances, is of great advantage.

THE UNIVERSAL MICROSCOPE.

List of Achromatic Object-glasses for the Universal Microscope.

Focal length.		Linear magnifying powers, nearly, with eyepieces		
		No. 1.	No. 2.	No. 3.
2 inches,	with ordinary body	20	30	65
	with lengthening tube	40	55	100
1 inch,	with ordinary body	55	75	155
	with lengthening tube	95	125	250
½ inch,	with ordinary body	115	150	325
	with lengthening tube	190	250	500
¼ inch,	with ordinary body	175	225	480
	with lengthening tube	275	350	650
⅛ inch,	with ordinary body	315	425	865
	with lengthening tube	470	630	1250

The higher powers, viz. the ½ inch, ¼ inch, and ⅛ inch, have no adjustments for variations in the thin glass or other media interposed between their front lenses and the object; but they are corrected for a piece of glass ·008 thick, and these object-glasses will define the best when the object is covered with glass of such measurement.

The forceps (fig. 41, O), a small pair of pliers (V), and a glass plate with a ledge (W) are also generally supplied with this microscope.

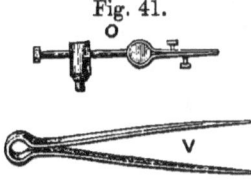

Fig. 41.

½ size.

The case is made of mahogany, and of an upright form; the instrument, when put away, slides into it so that the pillar occupies the left-hand corner next the door; the stand is blocked to prevent any injury in carriage. One object-glass and one eyepiece are intended to remain on the microscope; a small board on the door receives the remaining apparatus, with room for any additional object-glasses or eyepieces that may be required. Provision is also

H

made in the case for a small box (fig. 42), to contain the extra apparatus alluded to hereafter.

This microscope can be kept in perfect working order by a little attention to one or two parts. If the body work loose in its dovetail fitting, it can be corrected by unscrewing the screw (fig. 37, *a*) at the upper part of the limb half a turn, and by screwing up the one (*b*) at the lower part of the limb to the same extent; or if this should not be sufficient, it may be repeated until the body will not rock in its fitting. This operation is really that of pushing up by the lower screw, a dovetailed wedge; but, to retain this in its proper place, it is always necessary that the upper screw should also be screwed down firmly upon it.

The chain connected with the quick and slow movements may also work loose; if so, it can be tightened by carefully turning round from left to right the smaller screw-head (*c*) at the upper end of the limb.

The extra apparatus, which may be added to the instrument at any time without its being sent back to the makers, is common to the third as well as this class of microscopes, and is described in pages 83 to 88 inclusive; but the case for containing it is shown in the accompanying figure.

Fig. 42.

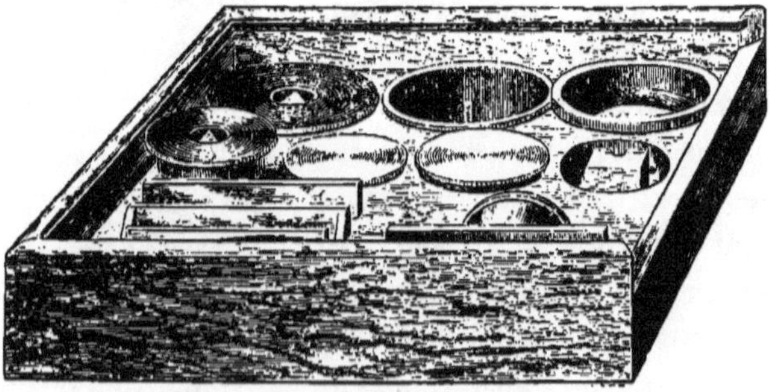

½ size.

Stage with Actions.

The double spring (fig. 37, I) which holds the stage-plate (K) can be removed by unscrewing; after this is done, the opening (P) will receive what is commonly called a Stage with actions (fig. 43); this is so contrived to fit on as to admit of its being turned round as a whole, and consequently always central with the body; or, in other words, during the rotation, the object will not move out of the field of view; the amount of movement at right angles is half an inch each way, and is effected by means of the milled heads (I, K); the object can be moved to and fro on the ledge (L), which slides up and down, and a small spring can be turned to clamp the object, when necessary.

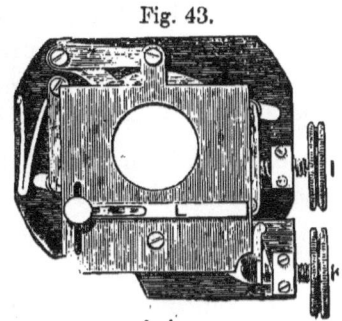

Fig. 43.

½ size.

The Combined Body.

This is a contrivance for the attachment of three object-glasses and three eye-pieces to the instrument at once (see fig. 44).

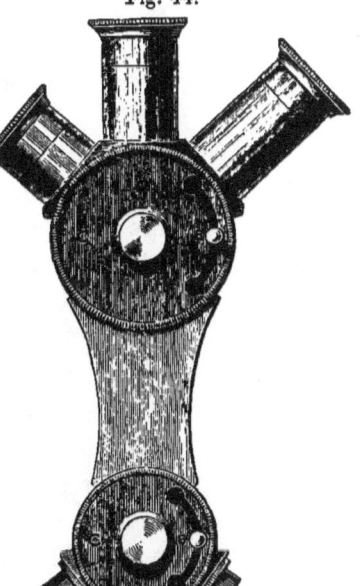

Fig. 44.

½ size.

Only one of each of these can be central with the axis of the body at the same time; but any of the others can be brought into the central position by pressing in the rounded head of the pin (B), when either of the disks (C) can be turned in the required direction, and will be stopped again by the pin (B) springing out.

This arrangement may be appreciated by those who are deterred from making a casual use of the microscope, either from the trouble of putting an instrument up, or from the delays which the necessary changes involve, whilst it will considerably assist in the investigation of objects which are undergoing a change either in their position or their structure, and when a great range of power is required with the least possible delay. As a luxury, it will apply to every use of the microscope.

Fig. 45.

½ size.

The change from the square body (fig. 37, E) to this one is made by unscrewing a large screw which is at the back of the dovetail piece fitting into the limb, and the body will then push off downwards. This process is, of course, reversed when a body has to be put on; but then some care must be taken that the screw in the lower end of the body fits the slot it slides into at the lower end of the dovetail piece, to effect which the screw may require either a little screwing up or unscrewing before the body is put on.

THE BINOCULAR BODY. 101

Wenham's Binocular Body for the Universal Microscope.

This Binocular Body (fig. 45), as applied to the Universal Microscope, possesses the following advantages:—The object-glasses are mounted on a rotating disk, as already described under the combined body; an adjustment for different distances between the eyes is made by turning the milled head (F), which will move the draw-tubes (E, E) up or down. The reflecting prism is placed close behind the back lens of each object-glass, and with this arrangement the field of view is not cut off when the objects are viewed as transparent, with the highest power.

The change to the binocular body can also be made with the same facility as has been already described under the "combined body."

Full directions for the use of Wenham's Binocular Body have been already given in pages 48 to 55, inclusive, of this treatise, and apply generally to this particular form of it.

SINGLE MICROSCOPES.

Darwin's Instrument.

An instrument and apparatus exactly similar to those shown in figs. 46 and 47 were made to the express design of Mr. Darwin, and it is with such arrangements that he has carried on many of his valuable investigations.

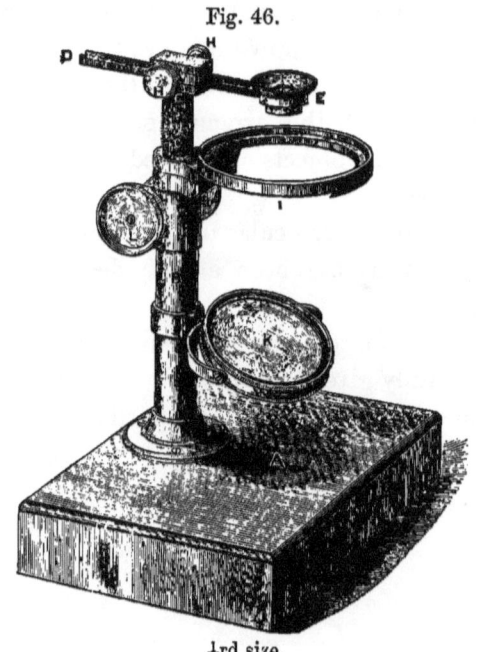

Fig. 46.

⅓rd size.

The base (fig. 46, A) is a stout block of oak or mahogany, near one edge of which is screwed an upright stem (B); into this is fitted a triangular bar (C), having a slight cross-arm attached at the top, to carry the magnifiers. This arm is provided with a fitting for rotation at C, or it can be moved backwards or forwards by turning either of the small

DARWIN'S SINGLE MICROSCOPE. 103

milled heads (H); and by using these movements, separately or combined, the magnifier may be moved over any part of an object which is placed upon the stage (I). The focus of the lenses is adjusted by turning either of the milled heads (L, L); and a large concave mirror, with a smaller flat one at its back, provided with all the necessary movements, supplies the means for transmitting light through an object.

Fig. 47.

⅓rd size.

Various pieces of apparatus, which may be required in dissection, fit into the stage of this instrument, which is prepared for the purpose with a deep recess. Into this will fit either of the two large saucers with glass bottoms (T, U); they differ in depth, but are both intended for the dissection of large objects in fluid; and in those cases where transmitted light is not required, the specimen may be pinned to a piece of cork (O), which is loaded with lead to keep it firmly at the bottom of the saucer.

For small objects the size of the stage may be reduced by

dropping into its recess the brass plate (R), which has a central aperture of only one inch and a half; and the following pieces of apparatus are provided of this size :—two flat and two concave glasses, a piece of boxwood covered with cork, and a holder (P) to receive the ordinary 3×1 glass plates.

Beneath the stage of the instrument is a dovetail fitting for the brass plate (M), which is provided with a small aperture, and serves as a diaphragm; or when the opening is closed by the small shutter (N), the brass plate forms a dark background for the stage.

The lenses are mounted so as to drop easily into the extremity (fig. 46, E) of the arm, and are generally either single lenses or Coddingtons; but Mr. Darwin recommends in addition a large doublet (fig. 47, S), the two lenses of which are mounted, so as to be used separately or in combination, and in this way to furnish three low powers. The small socket of the bent arm to which the doublet is attached fits the arm at the end (fig. 46, D) which is opposite to that part where the ordinary lenses drop in.

This instrument, which is generally termed Darwin's Dissecting Microscope, together with all the apparatus and some dissecting instruments, is carefully packed in a small mahogany case with a lock and handle.

AN IMPROVED SINGLE MICROSCOPE,

with or without a Binocular Arrangement to the Magnifiers.

Fig. 48.

⅓rd size.

The base (fig. 48, A) of this instrument is a square block of mahogany, with the upper edge and corners rounded off, and with four strong brass pillars (B) at the angles, which support, at a height of four inches from the table, a brass plate (C) six and a half inches square; above this are two circular brass plates, the first (D) of the same diameter as the square plate, with a revolving fitting at the centre, and the means of tightening it down underneath by a large milled head (E); the second and top plate of all (F) is much smaller, and is held down by springs, which allow it to be moved pleasantly over the lower plate to the extent of three-quarters of an inch in any direction; this is equivalent to a space at the centre of one inch and a half diameter, and of this size the opening (G) of the top stage is made for the reception of various glasses, troughs, or holders for dissection.

The magnifiers drop into the extremity of an arm (H) which comes in a diagonal direction from the left-hand back pillar; here it is fixed to a triangular bar (I) which can be moved up or down by a milled head (K) connected with a rack and pinion for the adjustment of the focus: the arm can be turned aside to the left, but in the other direction it stops when central with the revolving fitting of the first circular plate already alluded to.

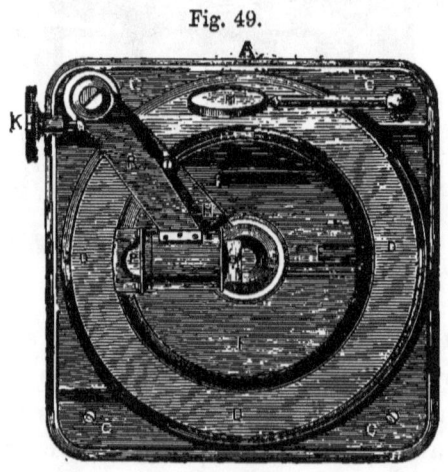

Fig. 49.

⅓rd size.

When light is required from below for transparent objects, a concave mirror (L), provided with a semicircle and other necessary fittings, can be turned up from a recess in the mahogany base, and a side condensing-lens (M), with ball-and-socket and other movements, supplies all necessary illumination from above.

In nearly all dissecting microscopes the magnifier is moved over the object, and consequently away from either condenser- or mirror-illumination. In this instrument the magnifying power is stationary; and not only does the illumination continue to be the same whilst the object is moved about in every direction, but any particular part that is being examined will remain in view whilst it is rotated by turning the larger circular brass plate (D).

The following are the advantages of this construction. The size or, as it might be termed, spread of the microscope gives great firmness, and also plenty of room on the top plates for the hands to rest upon during dissection.

The stand is comparatively low; for in a single microscope it is necessary to allow some considerable open space beneath the lowest part of the stage, to admit an illumination from below when the light in front is at a moderate elevation; but the unavoidable height is taken full advantage of in this instrument by giving a range of three inches and six-tenths to the rack of the triangular bar, and thus an object of considerable thickness may be placed under the magnifiers.

The Binocular Addition.

The binocular arrangement for this microscope is based upon the fact that, with single microscopes, when the object is in focus the rays emerge parallel from the magnifier; there is, therefore, on this account nothing to prevent the use of both eyes, one being close to the lens and the other some distance off: the size of the object will be the same in each instance, and the union of both images perfect.

This result is effected by the arrangement shown in figs. 48 and 49, half the aperture of the magnifier being allowed to proceed direct to one eye, whilst the other half is reflected by two L prisms (O, P) to the other eye. The two fields of view are unequal, and the space included in a small circle only is stereoscopic; but this result is no worse than the ordinary disadvantage of smallness of field common to all binocular single microscopes of moderate power; whereas the advantages which arise from employing reflecting prisms for one eye only are—much saving of light, only half the cost, and great facility in turning the prisms out of the way when one eye only is used.

The mounting required by this binocular arrangement is as follows:—To a semicylindrical tube (S) are attached two L prisms; one (o) is a fixture, but the other will slide in or out to suit the distances of different eyes; the two together are mounted upon a second arm (R) which fits immediately above the first arm, carrying the magnifier, and, when both eyes are used, the right-hand prism (o) should exactly cover one half of the magnifying lens.

The arm (R) is stopped when it reaches this position; but it can be turned out of the way to any extent in the other direction, and the fittings of the prisms allow of their easy removal when they require cleaning.

The apparatus supplied with this form of single microscope is very similar to that already described as belonging to Darwin's instrument. The brass saucers with glass bottoms are smaller; but a gutta-percha tray, to which any object may be pinned, is added for those specimens requiring dissection when in fluid; and the piece of cork, loaded with lead, is of an oblong form, and capable of being moved about upon the top stage-plate.

The case for the complete instrument is made of mahogany, and nearly all the spare room inside is made use of—a good-sized box for the dissecting instruments and apparatus being fitted between the four pillars of the instrument, and a narrow strip of wood for the magnifiers occupying the top right-hand corner.

Hand Magnifiers, with and without Stands.

No exact line of distinction can be drawn between this class of instruments and the single microscopes already described, because the various forms of hand magnifiers are frequently mounted upon some kind of stand; the stage for the object, if it require one, being extemporized in any way that may prove most convenient for the occasion. As examples of such arrangement, we give descriptions of the following instruments :—

The Patent Achromatic Binocular Magnifiers.

The great advantage secured by this arrangement of lenses is the employment of both eyes when using a magnifying power which, with an ordinary lens, would confine the observer to the use of one eye only.

Under these binocular magnifiers the object retains its natural or, as it is sometimes termed, stereoscopic appearance; the light, upon which definition mainly depends, is doubled; the magnifying power is apparently much increased; and the binocular lens will, as a rule, give a better result than a single one of double the magnifying power, without bringing any strain whatever upon the eyes.

The three sizes figured in Plate XXVIII., the foci of which are 7, 5, and 3 inches respectively, have also another advantage, in addition to those already enumerated, in being achromatic.

Directions for Use.

The lenses are plano-convex, and when in use the flat sides should always be placed next the eyes; and the mounting is so contrived that this may be done when the magnifiers are held in either hand.

As the distances of the eyes in different persons vary considerably, these lenses have a sliding fitting at A, by which the proper amount of separation may be obtained: the correct distance is easily determined by experiment; but, as a general rule, if a flat object appear convex, the lenses are too near together; or when too far apart, the same surface will appear concave,—the right distance being somewhere between.

It will be found by many, and especially those who have been accustomed to make constant use of a single lens, that these binocular magnifiers require at first some rather careful adjustment in holding them; for, besides the alteration of distance already described, the eyes must be directed vertically, upon the flat surfaces of the lenses; and each eye should see the object clearly defined. The former may be tested by slightly altering the position of the lenses, and watching whether the definition improve or otherwise; the latter by shutting each eye alternately, without moving the head or the magnifier.

Stand for Binocular Magnifiers.

For really careful work, and when neither hand is at liberty to hold the magnifier, some Stand is necessary, and one specially contrived for the purpose is shown in the Plate. The lenses, after the ordinary handles (B) are unscrewed, can be attached by means of the milled head (C) to the semicircular arm (D) fitting by a pin into the tube (E), which slides upon an inner rod (F), and this again rotates on a fitting at (G).

By this plan of mounting, the lenses can be placed in any necessary position, or any requisite change may be effected with ease and certainty. The adjustment for focus takes place on the vertical rod (H), a slow movement being given by the milled head (L); or if any great or quick alteration be necessary, the milled head is thrown out of gear by pressing in the lever (K), and the whole of the arm and its fittings can be moved rapidly up or down to any position on the rod (H), the mere act of releasing the lever fixing the arm again immediately in any place.

The Binocular principle as thus applied to single magnifiers is of course limited in power, and no lenses of shorter focus than 3 inches (the highest power here given) can be used in this way with advantage; but within their range it is quite impossible to enumerate all the purposes for which these lenses are peculiarly suitable.

Hand Magnifier.

The most generally useful form of hand magnifier, and one which may be carried in the pocket, is shown in fig. 50; it is provided with three lenses (*a, b, c*), the curvatures of which are so arranged as to admit of the powers being used separately or in combination, in this way furnishing seven different magnifying powers.

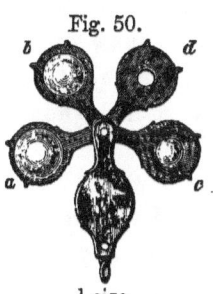

Fig. 50.

½ size.

The lenses are mounted in tortoiseshell frames together with a stop (*d*), which may be used with advantage to cut off some of the circumferential rays of the high powers. The smallest lens (*c*) is plano-convex, and, whether used separately or in combination, should always be held with its flat side towards the object. To use this or any other kind of hand magnifier with the greatest advantage, the lens should be kept as near to the eye as possible, the object being gradually brought into the focus.

Stand for Hand Magnifier.

This form of hand magnifier may also be attached to a very simple form of stand (fig. 51), which will convert it at once into a very useful and inexpensive dissecting instrument. To accomplish this, the tortoiseshell frame of the magnifiers is provided with a square metal socket, to fit a small arm with a sliding fitting upon a short stem, which is screwed at its lower end into a small circular base. The ordinary forceps of the compound microscope are also sometimes fitted to the rod of the same stand, and the various provisions for the movement of the object, or for the adjustment of focus, are so evident as to make any further description superfluous.

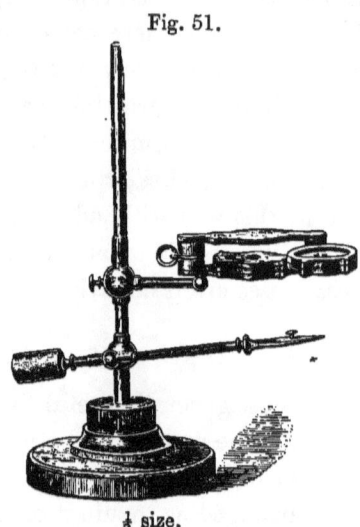

Fig. 51.

½ size.

Coddington Lenses.

Coddington lenses (fig. 52) are also employed as hand magnifiers; and although their foci are short, any one with a steady hand can use them easily. The mounting shown here is of an improved form, and meets the following requirements. When closed (see

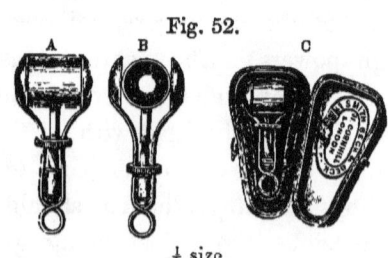

Fig. 52.

½ size.

DISSECTING INSTRUMENTS. 113

A), the surfaces of the lens are completely protected from any injury they might receive whilst kept in the pocket. If the Coddington be uncovered for use (see B), the convex surfaces project beyond the mounting, and cut off no light in the examination of an opaque object: the opening or closing is managed by moving the small milled head down or up the central stem; and this may be done with one hand, if the mounting be attached to a braid hung round the neck, or fastened to a waistcoat button.

The Coddington lenses vary in focus, and are mounted in German silver, aluminium-bronze, silver, or gold; one of the last kind is represented at C.

INSTRUMENTS USED IN DISSECTION.
Knives.
Fig. 53.

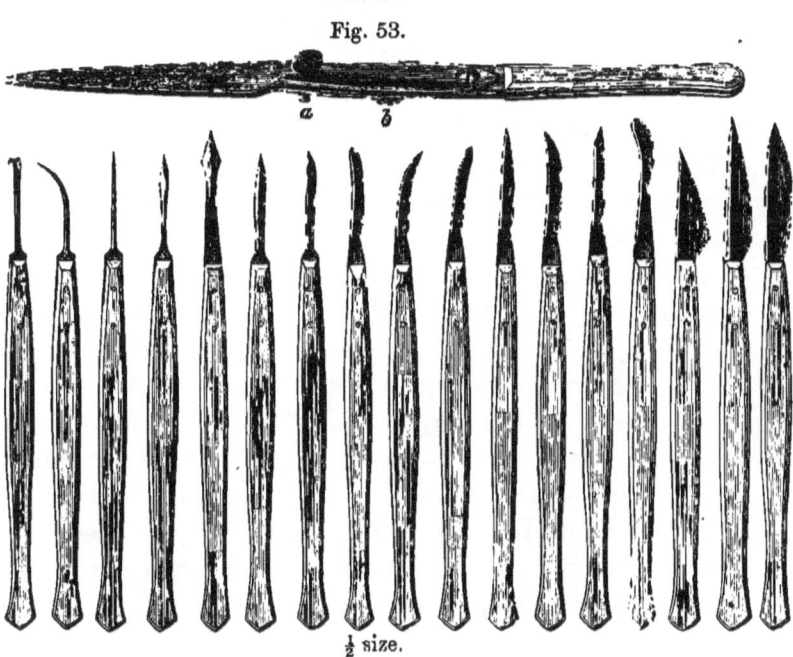

½ size.

I

The instruments which may be required in the process of dissection are very various. Only a few are shown in figs. 53, 54, and these require but little further explanation than that which is so evidently conveyed by the illustrations. The knife lying across in fig. 53 is known as Valentine's: the purpose for which it is contrived is that of making thin sections of soft substances by means of two blades, the distance between them, and, of course, the thickness of the section, being regulated by means of two screws (a, b); the former passes through both blades, the latter through one only, and pushes against the other, by which arrangement the parallelism of the blades can be maintained when they are more or less separated.

At the left-hand end of fig. 53 is shown a needle-holder, in which the needles may be stored at the end (d), or, when required for use, can be held firmly at the other end by pushing up the ring (c). The next illustration is that of a hook; and then follow curved and straight points which merge into knives, commencing with blades of lancet-shape and passing on to others of very various forms, any choice of which must be entirely dependent upon the service for which they are required.

It frequently occurs, when many of the subjects for dissection are very minute, that any definite cutting is impossible; and various devices have to be adopted for the separation of their various parts. Sometimes when these are sufficiently hard, they may be quickly and satisfactorily detached by two needle-points, after the entire specimen has been completely crushed; this process must, however, generally be done in some fluid and between two pieces of glass, so that the results of more or less pressure may be watched under the microscope.

DISSECTING INSTRUMENTS. 115

Scissors and Forceps.

The illustrations of the scissors and forceps in fig. 54 require even less comment than those of the knives. A form of spring scissors is shown at the top; and of the other three pairs, one has straight and the others have either curved or bent blades. Of the forceps, the pair nearest the scissors is

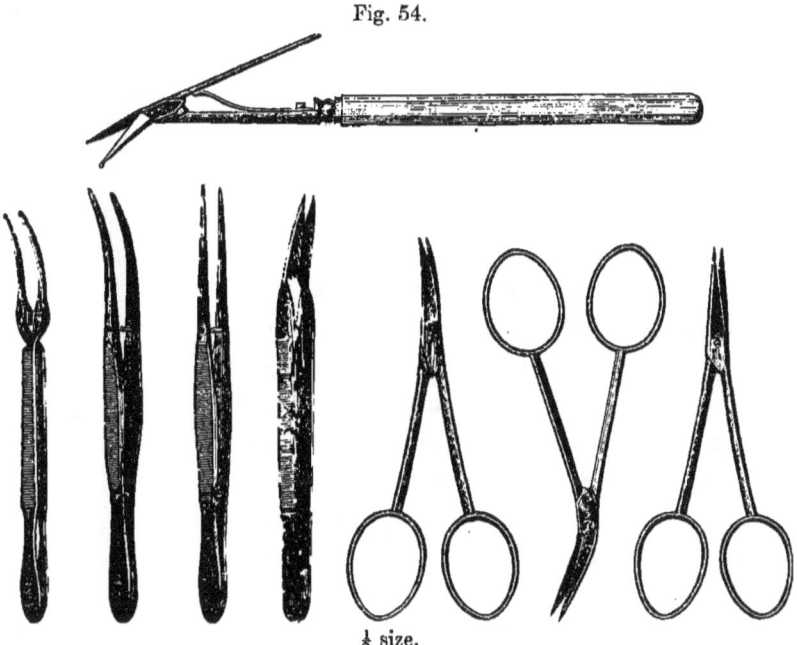

Fig. 54.

½ size.

supplied with cutting points; that at the left-hand end has crossed points which close by their own spring, and are separated by pressure lower down, exactly the reverse of ordinary forceps, two pairs of which are shown in the other illustrations, only differing from each other in the shape of their points.

I 2

Quekett's Forceps.

Another instrument which comes under the title of forceps is shown in fig. 55. It is a contrivance of the late Professor Quekett, not for the purposes of dissection, but for picking up anything which may be at some considerable depth in water. When in use, it is held by a thumb and two fingers, the upper loop being provided for the former and the two lower ones for the latter: if then the thumb be moved up or down, the outside tube of the forceps is raised or lowered, and this opens or closes the points at the lower end.

Improved Wood-cutting Machine.

This instrument is designed for making very thin sections of those substances which, either prepared or unprepared, may be cut with a sharp knife. The general appearance of the machine is that of a very short pillar (see figs. 56, 57), and it is made of iron, so that the top surface may be case-hardened; otherwise the cutting instrument would constantly catch on the surface of the metal and be injured.

In the centre of the machine, at the upper portion, a hole is carefully bored to receive one or other of the brass plugs, fig. 56 (*h, h*); when either of these is pushed down to the bottom of the hole, it comes upon a loose washer, the height of which is regulated by a fine

Fig. 55.

½ size.

screw (c), and the brass plug is prevented turning round by a slot in its side, which fits a pin in the iron hole.

The substance from which sections are required is placed in the central aperture of one of the brass plugs. The fitting of the material must be quite tight, and it is best to push it up from the lower end of the hole until it projects about $\frac{1}{10}$th of an inch from the upper end. The brass plug, when thus furnished, is placed in the machine, and pushed down until the projecting end of the substance to be cut is about level with the iron surface (*a, a*) of the machine.

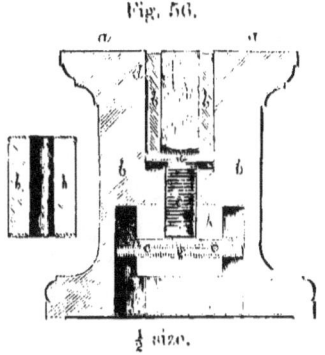

Fig. 56.

⅓ size.

In making a section (see fig. 57), the machine is held by the fingers of the left hand, whilst the cutting instrument, in the form of a large chisel, is grasped in the right hand, with the end of its handle pressed against the right shoulder, and the level of its edge resting on the case-hardened surface of the machine.

The chisel cannot be held too firmly; and whilst the right hand keeps it in position, it should be pushed forward by the shoulder, the thumb of the left hand giving it at the same time a side motion; so that, commencing to make the section with the right-hand corner of the chisel, and completing the cut with the other corner, the cutting edge is carried steadily and in an oblique direction across the material: for the purpose of making very thin sections, this is the most advantageous way in which any cutting edge can be employed.

After each cut with the chisel, the brass plug (*b*) containing the material is pushed up by the screw (*c*), its milled edge (*g*) being easily reached by a finger and thumb through the two openings in the sides of the iron pillar. The screw has fifty threads in an inch, and there are twenty divisions on its bevelled edge; therefore by using any side of the two

Fig. 57.

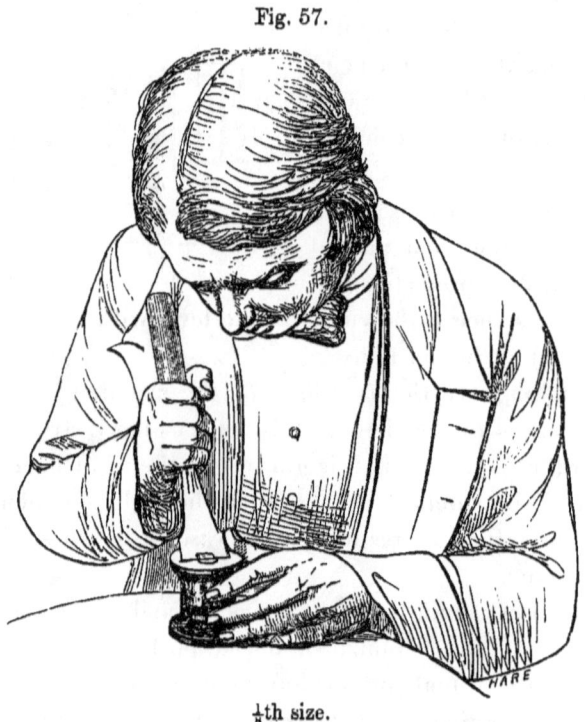

⅛th size.

openings just mentioned as an index, an exact upward movement of one thousandth of an inch or more is easily made, and can be repeated with certainty.

In making thin sections by any method, the chief difficulty is in the preparation of a very fine, sharp edge to the cutting instrument; and we have adopted the particular form already described, not only because we know that it is used in the trade with great success, but also because a careful carpenter or cabinet-maker can easily sharpen the chisel, if any person should find a difficulty in the matter.

Nearly all substances require some preparation before they can be properly sliced: woods and horns have to be soaked or sometimes even boiled in water before they become sufficiently soft; hairs are generally glued together in a bundle, or they are drawn quite tightly into a piece of cork or soft wood; whilst other substances will not offer sufficient resistance to the edge of the knife until they are hardened. Under such a variety of circumstances no very definite rules can be established; and, after all that might be done, there is no instruction equal to that which may be obtained by being thrown upon one's own ingenuity.

INSTRUMENTS USED IN MOUNTING OBJECTS.

Glass and other Slips.

The specimens or preparations intended to be kept as permanent objects are now almost universally placed on slips of glass, wood, or tin, measuring three inches by one inch. The first material is by far the most frequently employed, and these slips are generally of plate or crown glass with the edges ground; but rough edges as left from the diamond-cut are no disadvantage when the slides are covered with paper.

Cutting Diamond.

The glass slips are now so easily obtained at moderate prices that it is seldom any person finds it advantageous to cut them up for himself; but, if otherwise, a glazier's diamond (fig. 58) is the best instrument for the purpose, and after a little practice in holding the diamond at the proper angle, there is no difficulty in cutting the glass so as to leave a tolerably smooth edge.

Fig. 58. Fig. 59.

Thin Glass.

It is an almost invariable practice to cover the object with very thin glass; this material comes from the manufacturers in small, angular-shaped sheets, which require careful cutting by a diamond (fig. 59) to bring them into suitable sizes and shapes, the most frequent forms being circles or squares of not less than three nor more than nine tenths of an inch, with all the intermediate gradations in tenths; there are, however, frequent cases in which oblong or oval pieces are required, and there is no difficulty in obtaining them.

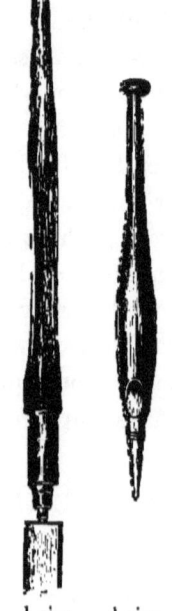

½ size. ½ size.

The Disk-cutter.

Fig. 60.

An instrument for cutting small circles of thin glass is shown in fig. 60, and is used in the following manner:—The central inner stem (a) is held in an upright position upon the piece of thin glass by the forefinger of the left hand, so that there is a gentle pressure at the small base (e), which is padded with cork, and round this the diamond (d) is rotated by turning the tube (f) with the thumb and finger of the right hand, from which also must be given at the same time the necessary pressure for the cut of

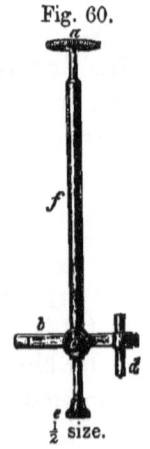

½ size.

the diamond. This operation may be repeated over a large piece of glass, after which, a slight bending of the glass backwards and forwards will develope the various annular cracks; and when these are fairly through the thickness of the glass, the disks or circles are released by carefully breaking away in pieces the thin glass surrounding them.

By means of the transverse sliding arm (*b*) the diamond is readily adjusted for cutting circles of any required diameter; and the small milled head (*c*) is used to fix the arm securely at any part of the range.

The same diamond may also be used in cutting the thin glass into squares, for which purpose some small wooden rules only are required.

The Mounting of Objects.

There are various ways of preserving microscopic objects: many may be mounted, as it is termed, " dry," which implies that the specimen is merely covered with a piece of glass as a protection from injury or dust; or when the specimen will not bear any pressure, it is usual to employ a ring of card or paper to carry the thin glass. The dry plan is usually adopted with sections of bones or teeth, hairs, feathers, scales of insects, sections of recent woods, fructification of ferns, some of the Diatomaceæ, zoophytes, small shells, and many other objects.

Mounting-Media.

The purpose for which preparations are mounted in a medium of some kind, is either to preserve the specimen or to make it more transparent. But in many cases both of these results may be required; for instance, many of the Diatomaceæ, spicules and gemmules of sponges and Gorgonias, sections of *Echinus*-spines, some of the Foraminifera, &c.,

cannot be well examined by transmitted light until they are rendered more transparent by some medium; whilst other preparations require, in addition, the preserving property of the material, such as minute insect-dissections, *Acari* and parasites, the finest injected preparations, many crystals and polarizing objects.

It is therefore impossible to establish any definite rules; but it will be found that the best course of proceeding may easily be determined by experiment.

Canada Balsam.

Of the various media, Canada balsam is perhaps more frequently employed than any other in mounting objects; it is generally used in a semifluid state, or, if necessary, it may be made more fluid by mixing turpentine or chloroform with it.

The material itself, although generally supplied in a bottle such as is shown in fig. 62, is best kept for general

Fig. 61. Fig. 62.

½ size.

use in a bottle with a ground cap (see fig. 61), and the

quantity that is required for use may be taken out by the glass dipping-rod.

Brass Table and Lamp.

With Canada balsam some amount of heat is almost always required, either previously to the object being placed in it, or afterwards, to harden it sufficiently, and prevent any alteration or shifting of the specimen; under such circumstances it is best to place the slide upon a small brass table, with a spirit-lamp underneath (see fig. 63); in general

Fig. 63.

½ size.

only a slight warmth is required, and sufficient heat will be communicated by the brass top of the table when the flame of the spirit-lamp is quite small. If, however, under any circumstances any greater heat be required, the object may be placed so as to be over the small opening near the end of the table, with the lamp immediately underneath. It must nevertheless be borne in mind that air-bubbles are produced by the boiling or overheating of the balsam, and also, from the same cause, the balsam will turn of a brown colour and become very brittle.

Page's Forceps.

Another method of warming a slide is by merely moving it backwards and forwards across the flame of a spirit-lamp; and if by this plan the glass should become too warm to hold in the fingers, Page's forceps (fig. 64) may be employed. The wood of which the sides of these are made will not conduct the heat, so that whilst the slide is placed at one extremity

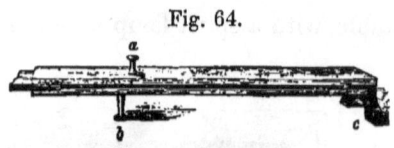

Fig. 64.

and submitted to any amount of temperature, the other end of the forceps may be held in the hand with impunity. The sides of the forceps are separated by pressing the pins (a, b); and to let the slide cool without coming in contact with any cold surface which might crack it, the forceps, together with the slide, will stand upon a table in the position shown by the drawing.

Some of the conditions connected with the employment of Canada balsam, such as its high refractive power, the heat required in its use, and its not amalgamating with an object unless perfectly dry or saturated with a solvent, entirely prevent its use in the preservation of many objects; there are, however, other and valuable substitutes.

Deane's Medium.

Deane's gelatine medium requires much less heat than Canada balsam, and is admirably suited to objects in a moist state. The following directions for its use are given by Mr. Deane upon the bottles in which he usually supplies it:—

"Set the bottle in water sufficiently hot to liquify the medium perfectly, and then with a piece of quill-glass tube, made warm by being immersed at one end in hot water, take up a portion of the medium, and drop it on the object previously arranged in its place on a warm glass-slip, and then cover with its appropriate thin glass, also made warm, lest the jelly set before the operation is completed. A pewter hot-water plate answers well for warming the glass.

"Objects to be mounted in this medium should be quite moist and free from air-bubbles; some may be floated into their places in water, or weak spirit and water, the superfluous moisture being drained away by tilting on end, and then with bibulous paper or a cambric handkerchief. Care must be taken to prevent the object becoming dry before the medium is put to it."

Farrants' Medium.

Farrants' medium is composed of gum and glycerine: it requires no warmth whatever in its use, and is usually kept in a semifluid state; but a small quantity of it will become tough on exposure to the air for about an hour, if it be made in the right proportions.

This material is admirably suited for many kinds of preparations, more especially for moist specimens, and for small objects living in either air or water.

Glass and other Cells.

The three substances already mentioned, Canada balsam, Deane's medium, and Farrants' medium, form not only the materials in which the objects are mounted, but also the cements for keeping the covering (thin glass) in its proper place upon the slide. This cannot be the case with many mounting materials, of which the following may be mentioned as possessing valuable preservative properties:—dilute spirits of wine, distilled water, Goadby's fluid, Thwaites's fluid, a solution of chloride of zinc, and castor-oil.

To confine such materials as these, it is almost always necessary to make a cell of some substance upon which they cannot act as solvents, and a mixture of asphalt and gold-size may generally be employed for this purpose, or either of them may be used alone; but the former often proves too brittle, and the latter takes some time to harden. Asphalt or gold-size is generally supplied in bottles the same as that shown in fig. 62; but the gold-size is considered by some persons to be more convenient for use when kept in a small metal tube shown in fig. 65.

Fig. 65.

½ size.

Cell-machine.

Fig. 66.

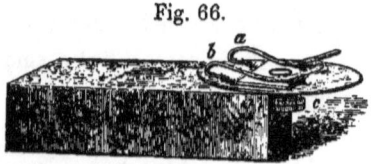

The cells of either or both of the materials just mentioned are best made by means of the instrument shown in fig. 66. The slide is held on the small circular plate by the two springs (a, b), and whilst the right hand, resting on the wood block, holds a camel's-hair pencil containing the cell-mate-

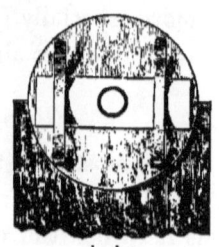

½ size.

rial, the circular brass table is spun round by quickly passing a finger of the left hand over the small milling (c) underneath; a thin ring of the material is thus painted on the slide, and the thickness of the cell is regulated by the number of the coats, each of which should be allowed some time to dry before another is added.

After the cell is made and is sufficiently hard, the object, together with the mounting-material, are placed in it and covered with a piece of thin glass; the superfluous mounting-material is soaked up by blotting-paper or some other means, and a few additional coats of the cell-material are added at and over the edge of the covering-glass to permanently seal the preparation.

Glass Cells.

The method of cell-making just described is only available with objects of very moderate thickness; but if a clean, secure, and moderately deep cell be required, there is no material equal to glass.

Fig. 67.

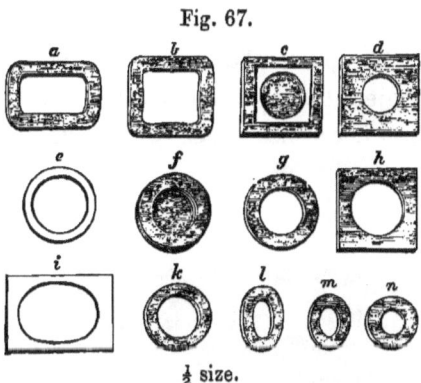

½ size.

A few of different sizes are shown in fig. 67: c and f have solid bottoms, and e and i are made from the microscopic thin glass; the others are sections of different kinds of glass tube, and may be had of any thickness.

All glass cells are generally cemented to the glass slips with marine glue. This material is usually supplied in small pieces packed in a bottle similar to fig. 62; but, when required for use, thin slices are placed between the cell and the glass slips, and whilst exposed to considerable warmth the cell is pressed down hard, so as to come in as close contact as possible with the glass slip. The superfluous marine glue is easily removed with a knife when the slide is cold. Although marine glue is invariably the best cement for fastening the cell to the glass slip, gold-size and asphalt will answer perfectly in securing the thin glass cover and sealing up the cell.

Labels.

When a slide requires covering with paper after the object has been mounted, the labels (fig. 68) may be used to give a neat finish; and the gummed square labels (fig. 69), ruled with six faint lines, give considerable space for writing the name or any other particulars connected with the preparation. If the object be not covered with paper, it is usual to write upon the unoccupied spaces of the glass slips with the diamond shown in fig. 59.

Fig. 68.   Fig. 69.

True size.   True size.

COLLECTING-BOTTLES. 129

Small Glass Bottles.

For the preservation of some kinds of microscopic objects Dr. Guy has recommended the use of small flattened glass bottles (fig. 70), and they may answer well under some circumstances, whilst in other cases the irregularities and imperfections of the glass will be found to obstruct most annoyingly the best definition of an object-glass.

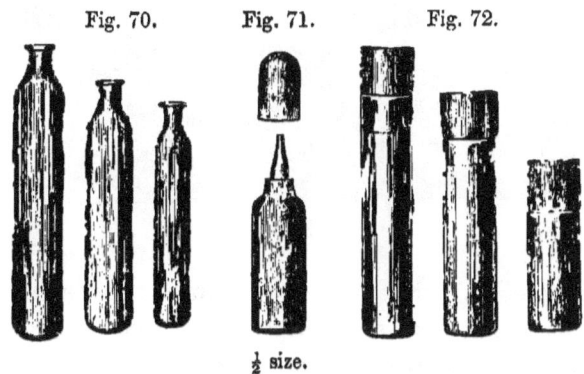

Fig. 70.   Fig. 71.   Fig. 72.

½ size.

In the dissection or other preparation of microscopic objects, reagents or other fluids may be occasionally required in small quantities, and in such cases bottles similar to the one shown in fig. 71 may be used. The tapering mouth-piece (which is removable for the introduction of the fluid into the bottle) only permits a small quantity to escape at a time, and the ground-glass cap, when fitted over the neck, excludes dust and prevents evaporation.

The bottles shown in fig. 72 are used in collecting specimens, for which purpose they are exceedingly convenient; three sizes are represented in the illustration, which so fully explains their capabilities that any further description would be superfluous.

K

Case for Instruments and Materials.

Fig. 73.

⅓rd size.

The materials and instruments required at different times in the preparation of microscopic objects are so numerous as frequently to run the chance of being mislaid. Such a circumstance might be most inconvenient; it is therefore a common plan to have them all arranged and packed in a mahogany case: the one shown in fig. 73 is of intermediate size, and illustrates the fitting of the top tray only; but this lifts out, because the space underneath is also fitted up for the reception of various articles.

Cabinets for Microscopic Objects.

The cabinets or boxes for holding microscopic objects are very various; but the best are those in which the specimens lie flat, as this position not only materially helps to preserve the preparations which are in fluid, but it greatly assists in the arrangement of a collection; and an object is much more easily found when lying flat than when placed on edge.

CABINETS FOR OBJECTS. 131

Fig. 74.

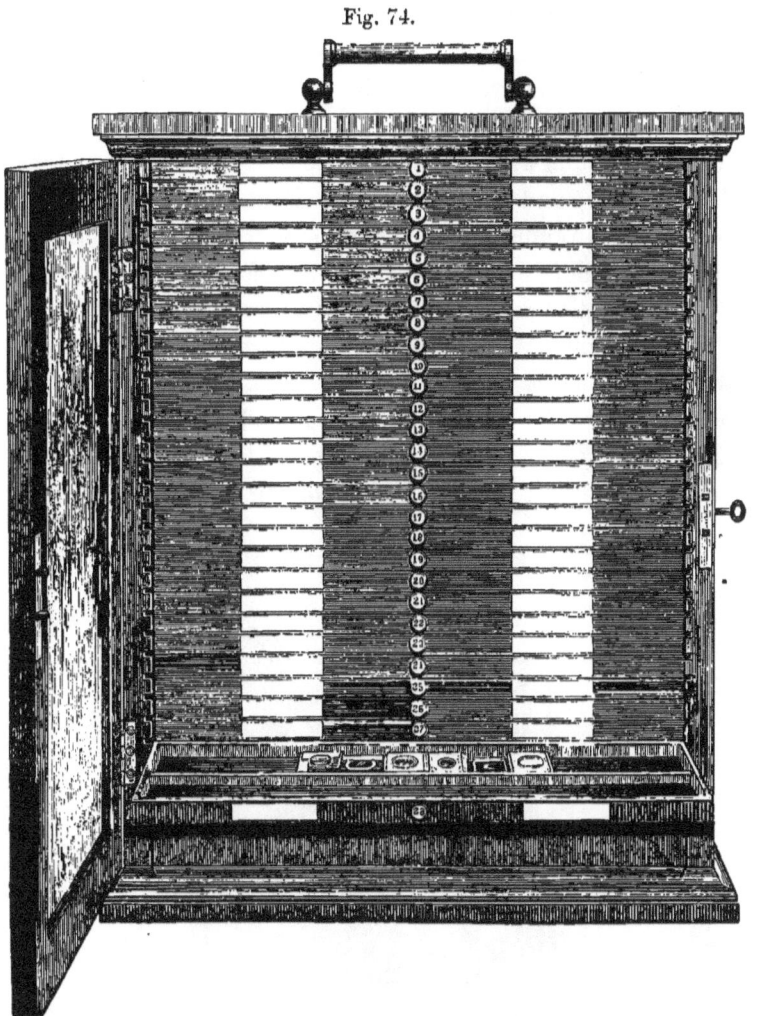

¼th size.

One of the best cabinets, with twenty-eight drawers, to hold 1000 objects, is shown in fig. 74; each drawer is divided into

three compartments by two partitions, which prevent the slides shifting backwards or forwards and becoming mixed when the drawers are moved in and out. The bottom of each drawer is made of strong paper, a material much superior in such a position to wood, which has always a tendency to warp and twist the work. Each drawer has in front two porcelain labels, which can be written upon in ink or pencil; and both are easily rubbed out, so that any record of the classification is readily made or altered.

Similar cabinets for objects are also made of a smaller size than that just described; but the workmanship of all has necessarily to be of the best kind, and when two of the same size differ in price it is because of the amount of work on the outside case, or the quality of the wood.

Quarto Cabinet.
Fig. 75.

¼th size.

QUARTO CABINET.   133

The "Quarto Cabinet" for objects, when closed, somewhat resembles a book composed of five thick leaves, which at a short distance from the edges are recessed on both sides (see fig. 75). The two outside surfaces are covered with leather; but the inner ones are lined with velvet, and narrow elastic, stretched rather tightly, is pinned down at intervals, so as to hold each object securely and separately (see fig. 76). This case will contain 144 specimens; and besides the choice that this plan admits of keeping the objects flat or on edge, according to the position in which the case is kept, the slides require no packing of any kind before they can be carried about, the elastic holding each object firmly in its place, and the leaves being fastened together by two double hooks, which, turning on a centre in the edge of the middle leaf, pass over two pins on the outside leaves.

Fig. 76.

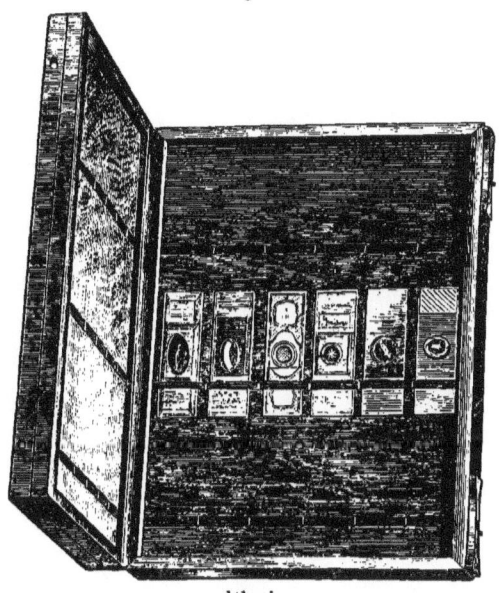

¼th size.

All the cases, smaller than those already described for containing objects, are provided with racks, and the better ones are made of mahogany to hold six dozen objects; but the commonest are made of deal or card, covered with cloth, and the usual sizes are those containing two dozen, one dozen, or half-a-dozen.

Microscopic Objects.

Specimens for the Microscope, so prepared as to be permanent, have now become a very large and important adjunct to the Microscope. The subject is too extensive to enter upon in this treatise; but we may mention that we have been engaged for some time past in making complete lists of microscopic objects: two or three of these are already published, and it is probable that we may complete the catalogue in the course of a year or so.

LIST OF ILLUSTRATIONS.

FRONTISPIECE.

Podura Scale, as shown by five different Object-glasses with No. 3 Eyepiece.

PLATE II.

First-class Microscope. Fig. 1, No. 1 Stand. Fig. 2, Diaphragm of Stage and fitting. Fig. 3, Draw-tube of Body.

PLATE III.

First-class Microscope, No. 2 Stand. Woodcut of Lever Stage.

PLATE IV.

Second-class Microscope. Fig. 1, No. 3 Stand. Fig. 2, Plain Stage to ditto.

PLATE V.

Eyepieces, Nos. 1, 2, 3. Fig. 4, Erecting-glass. Eight Object-glasses, viz. 2-inch, $1\frac{1}{2}$-in., $\frac{2}{3}$-in., $\frac{4}{10}$-in., $\frac{1}{4}$-in., $\frac{1}{5}$-in., $\frac{1}{8}$-in., $\frac{1}{20}$-in.

PLATE VI.

Achromatic Condenser, first- and second-class, and with and without diaphragm. Right-angle Prism; Wenham's Parabolic Reflector; Nachet's Prism; Amici's Prism; Instruments for measuring apertures of Object-glasses.

PLATE VII.

The Podura Scale as a test; *Pleurosigma quadratum*, as shown by oblique illumination and by Achromatic Condenser; *Navicula rhomboides*, as illuminated by Amici's Prism.

PLATE VIII.

Nobert's Lines, as shown by $\frac{1}{8}$ Object-glass and No. 3 Eyepiece, with oblique illumination.

Plate IX.

Fig. 1. A, B, C, and D, *Pleurosigma formosum*, as seen under various illuminations. Fig. 2, *Pleurosigma formosum*, as seen with a low power under oblique illumination. Figs. 3, 4, 5, 6, and 7, cast skin from head of Silkworm, to show use of Disk-revolver.

Plate X.

Apparatus used when objects are illuminated from above: Side Condensing Lenses and Reflector; Lieberkuhns; Dark Wells and Holder; Forceps; Disk-revolver.

Plate XI.

Splinter of Lucifer-match, and Podura Scale, illuminated from above.

Plate XII.

Tarsus of Spider (*Tegenaria atrica*) and Pigeon's feather, illuminated from above.

Plate XIII.

Arachnoidiscus Japonicus on marine plant, as seen by Lieberkuhn illumination with $\frac{1}{4}$-in. object-glass.

Plate XIV.

Polycystina from Barbadoes, as shown by " Dark-field " illumination.

Plate XV.

The new Halfpenny Coin of the Realm, as seen under the Erecting-glass.

Plate XVI.

Polarizing Apparatus, as applied to the Microscope: Nicol's Prisms; Black Glass and Thin Glass Polarizers; Selenite Plates; Double-image Prisms; Tourmaline; Crystal fittings, &c.

Plate XVII.

Objects seen under polarized light: Crystals of sulphate of copper and magnesia; Rhinoceros horn, oblique section; tendon of Ostrich, section; Crystallized salicine.

Plate XVIII.

Illustrations of experiments with Double-image Prisms, &c.

LIST OF ILLUSTRATIONS.

PLATE XIX.
Structure of the Scales of *Lepisma saccharina*.

PLATE XX.
Wenham's Binocular Body, for Achromatic Microscope.

PLATE XXI.
Live Boxes; Glass Troughs; Compressors; Frog Plate; Glass Plate with ledge; Glass Tubes.

PLATE XXII.
Micrometers; Camera Lucida; Quekett's Indicator; Leeson's Goniometer; Double and Quadruple Nosepieces.

PLATE XXIII.
Lamps and Revolving Table for the Microscope.

PLATE XXIV.
Head and thorax of *Demodex folliculorum*; and stinging-hairs of Nettle, as seen under the one-twentieth Object-glass.

PLATE XXV.
Mahogany Case for Large Best Microscope.

PLATE XXVI.
Apparatus Boxes, as packed for a complete Large Best Microscope.

PLATE XXVII.
Best Student's Microscope and Apparatus, in case; movable Stand for Microscope and Lamp.

PLATE XXVIII.
Patent Achromatic Binocular Magnifiers and Stand.

LIST OF WOODCUTS.

FIG.				PAGE
1.	Front of object-glass to explain adjustment of high powers			13
2.	Diagram to show the best relative positions of lamp and ∟ prism			14
3.	Sketch of feather, showing the component parts			31
4.	Diagram of form and structure of *Arachnoidiscus Japonicus*			33
5.	,,	to illustrate experiment with Lepisma-scales		51
6.	,,	of drop of water in live-box		55
7.	,,	to show position of eye when Camera Lucida is used		61
8.	,,	of crystals, to explain use of Leeson's Goniometer		66
9.	Maltwood's Finder			67
10.	Diagram of one square of Maltwood's Finder			68
11.	Popular Microscope: inclined position of stand			76
12.	,,	,,	vertical ditto	77
13.	,,	,,	horizontal ditto	79
14.	,,	,,	diaphragm of stage	79
15.	,,	,,	side condenser on stand	79
16.	,,	,,	forceps of stage	79
17.	,,	,,	glass plate with ledge, and thin glass cover	80
18.	,,	,,	pliers	80
19.	,,	,,	lower removable tray	81
20.	,,	,,	upper ditto, for apparatus	81
21.	,,	,,	mechanical stage	83
22.	,,	,,	achromatic condenser	84
23.	,,	,,	Lieberkuhn for 1-inch object-glass	84
24.	,,	,,	dark well	84
25.	,,	,,	section of parabolic reflector	84
26.	,,	,,	parabolic reflector	85
27.	,,	,,	polarizing apparatus	86
28.	,,	,,	diagram to explain use of Camera Lucida	87
29.	,,	,,	micrometer	88

LIST OF WOODCUTS.

FIG.				PAGE
30.	Popular Microscope:		live box	88
31.	,,	,,	glass trough	88
32.	Educational Microscope, as taken out of its case			89
33.	,,	,,	when set up for use	90
33a.	,,	,,	supplementary stage	90
34.	,,	,,	diaphragm of stage	91
35.	,,	,,	forceps of stage	91
36.	,,	,,	tray of extra apparatus	92
37.	Universal Microscope			94
38.	,,	,,	diaphragm of stage	95
39.	,,	,,	object-glasses	96
40.	,,	,,	eyepieces	96
41.	,,	,,	forceps of stage, pliers, and glass plate	97
42.	,,	,,	box of extra apparatus	98
43.	,,	,,	mechanical stage	99
44.	,,	,,	combined body	99
45.	,,	,,	binocular body	100
46.	Darwin's single Dissecting Microscope			102
47.	,,	,,	saucers and other apparatus	103
48.	Improved single Dissecting Microscope			105
49.	,,	,,	as seen from above	106
50.	Hand magnifiers in tortoiseshell			111
51.	,,	,,	on stand	112
52.	Coddington lenses			112
53.	Dissecting instruments; knives, points, hooks, and needle-holder			113
54.	,,		scissors and forceps	115
55.	Quekett's forceps			116
56.	Wood-cutting machine			117
57.	,,		in use	118
58.	Diamond for cutting thick glass			120
59.	,,	for writing or cutting thin glass		120
60.	Disk-cutter for thin glass			120
61.	Stoppered bottle for Canada balsam			122
62.	Ordinary bottle for mounting materials			122
63.	Brass table and lamp for mounting objects			123
64.	Page's forceps			124
65.	Metal tube containing gold size			126

LIST OF WOODCUTS.

FIG.		PAGE
66.	Cell-machine	126
67.	Glass cells	127
68.	Labels for covering objects	128
69.	Name-labels	128
70.	Flattened glass bottle for preserving objects	129
71.	Small stoppered bottle for reagents	129
72.	Small collecting-bottles	129
73.	Case for mounting materials and instruments	130
74.	Best cabinet for 1000 objects	131
75.	Quarto cabinet for objects, outside	132
76.	,, ,, inside	133

INDEX.

A.

Aberration—
   Chromatic 12
   Spherical 12
Achromatic Condenser:—
   First-class 10
   Second-class 11
   Third-class 83
Achromatic Microscope:—
   Construction of 1
   First- and Second-class 1
   Third-class 73
   Fourth-class 93
   Binocular 48
Adjustment for high powers 13, 16
Amici Prism 20
Aperture—
   of Object-glasses 4, 17
   measurement of 18
Apparatus:—
   Tray, third-class 92
   Box, fourth-class 98

B.

Balsam, Canada 122
Bases of Microscopes, revolving and folding 3
Binocular Microscope, Wenham's .. 48
Binocular body, fourth-class 101
Binocular Single Microscope 107
Binocular Hand Magnifiers 109
Bottles, small glass—
   for mounting objects 129
   for reagents 129
   for collecting objects 129
Bull's-eye Condenser 23

C.

Cabinets for objects 130
Camera Lucida:—
   First- and Second-class 61
   Third- and Fourth-class 86
Canada balsam 122
Cases for Microscopes:—
   First-class 70
   Second-class 71
   Popular Microscope 81
Cases for mounting-materials 130
Cast skin, head of Silkworm 28
Cell-machine 126
Cells of glass, for mounting objects 127
Coddington Lenses 112
Collecting-bottles 129
Combined body, of Universal Microscope 90
Compressor—
   Lever 57
   Reversible 58
   Wenham's 58
Condenser, Achromatic:—
   First- and Second-class 10
   Third-class 83
Condenser, Bull's-eye 23
Condenser, side 23
Construction of Achromatic Microscope 1
Crystals—
   of Sulphate of Copper and Magnesia 39
   to show rings 47

D.

Dark-field illumination 34

INDEX.

Darker's selenite plates 40
Dark wells:—
   First- and Second-class 25
   Third- and Fourth-class 84
Darwin's single Dissecting Microscope 102
Deane's medium 124
Demodex folliculorum 6
Diamond, cutting 119
Diaphragm of Stage:—
   First- and Second-class 9
   Third-class 91
   Fourth-class 95
Diaphragm of Achromatic Condenser 11
Directions for use of Microscope .. 8
Disk-cutter for thin glass 120
Dissecting Microscope:—
   Darwin's 102
   Improved 105
Dissecting-instruments 113
Draw-tube 4

E.
Educational Microscope 89
Erecting-glass 36
Errors in workmanship 22
Extra apparatus, fourth-class 98
Eyepieces 3
   of Universal Microscope 96

F.
Farrants' medium 125
Feather of Pigeon 31
Finder, Maltwood's 66
Flatness of field 17
Forceps for stage:—
   First- and Second-class 26
   Third-class 79
   Fourth-class 97
Forceps—
   Three-pronged 27
   Page's 124
   Quekett's 116
Frog plate 60

G.
Glass cells 127

Glass, thin 120
Glass, slips 119
Goniometer, Leeson's 65

H.
Halfpenny, the new 37
Hand Magnifiers 109, 111
   Binocular 109
   Stand for 112
High powers, adjustment of 13

I. J.
Illumination—
   oblique 20
   from above 23
   dark-field 34
Indicator, Quekett's 65
Jackson's Micrometers 63
Juncus conglomeratus, section of .. 62

K.
Kellner's Eyepiece 90
Knife, Valentine's 114

L.
Labels for covering objects 128
Lamps for Microscope 68
Lamp and table for mounting objects 123
Leeson's Goniometer 65
Lenses—
   Side condensing 23
   Coddington 112
Lepisma saccharina, scales of 49
Lever compressor 57
Lieberkuhns 25
Light, management of 8
"Lined" objects as tests 19
Lines, Nobert's 19
Live-boxes 55
   Live-box, " Screw" 57
   Third- and Fourth-class 88
Lucifer-match, splinter of 29

M.
Machine—
   for making sections of wood .. 116
   for making cells 120

# INDEX.

	Page		Page
Magnifiers, Hand	109	Object-glasses, list of first-class	5
Patent Achromatic Binocular	109	One-twentieth	6
Magnifying power—		Popular series	74
linear	4	Universal series	96
to ascertain	63	Tests for	12
Maltwood's Finder	66	Objects—	
Management of light	8	Mounting of	121
Measurement—		Labels for	128
of objects by Camera Lucida	62	Cabinets for	130
by micrometers	63	Quarto Cabinet for	132
Mechanical stage—		for Microscope	134
of Popular Microscope	83	Oblique illumination	20
of Universal Microscope	90	Opaque objects	23
Medium—		Opaque Disk-revolver	27
Deane's	124		
Farrants'	125	P.	
Micrometers, Jackson's	63	Page's Forceps	124
Microscopes, Achromatic:—		Parabolic Reflector, Wenham's:—	
First- and Second-class	1	First- and Second-class	34
Third-class	73	Third-class	84
Popular	73	Pigeon, feather of	31
Educational	89	*Pleurosigma quadratum*	19
Universal	93	*Pleurosigma formosum*	21
Microscopes, single:—		*Podura*, scale of	14
Darwin's	102	Polarized light	37
Improved	105	Polarizing apparatus, third- and	
Microscope Cases:—		fourth-class	86
First-class	70	*Polycystina* from Barbadoes	36
Second-class	71	Popular Microscope	73
Microscope Lamps	68	Prism—	
Microscope Table	69	Right-angle	10
Microscopic objects	134	Amici's	20
Mirror, use of	2, 9	Nachet's	20
Mounting of objects	121		
		Q.	
N.		Quadruple Nosepiece	65
Nachet's Prism	20	Quarto cabinet for objects	132
Navicula rhomboides	19	Quekett's Indicator	65
Nicol's Prism	38	Quekett's Forceps	116
Nobert's Lines	19		
Nosepiece—		R.	
Double	65	Reflector, side silver	24
Quadruple	65	Reversible compressor	58
		Right-angle prism	10
O.			
Object-glasses	3	S.	
Focal length of	4	Scale of *Lepisma saccharina*	49
Aperture of	4	Scale of *Podura*	14

INDEX.

Screw—
    Universal.................. 6
    Live-box 57
Selenite plates 40
    Darker's 40
Side silver reflector 24
Side condensing-lenses 23
    Third-class 79
Silkworm, cast skin of head...... 28
Single dissecting Microscope :—
    Darwin's 102
    Improved.................. 105
    Binocular 107
Slips, glass 119
Spider, tarsus of 30
Splinter of lucifer-match 29
Stage of Microscope 2
Stinging-hairs of *Urtica dioica*.... 8
Substage 2
Sulphate of copper and magnesia, crystals of 39

T.

Table for Microscope 69
Table and lamp for mounting objects........................ 123
Tarsus of Spider................ 30

Tests—
    for object-glasses 12, 23
    "Lined," objects as 19
Thin glass 129
Thin glass disk-cutter 120
Tourmalines 43
Trough......................... 56

U. V.

Universal screw 6
Universal Microscope 93
    Mechanical stage of 99
    Combined body of 99
    Binocular body of 101
Urtica dioica, stinging-hairs of.... 8
Use of Microscope, directions for.. 8
Valentine's knife 114

W.

Wenham's mode of measuring aperture 18
Wenham's Parabolic Reflector.... 34
Wenham's Binocular Microscope.. 48
Wenham's Compressor 58
Wood-cutting machine 116
Workmanship, errors in 22

THE END.

Printed by Taylor & Francis, Red Lion Court, Fleet Street.

DESCRIPTION OF FRONTISPIECE.

THE PODURA-SCALE.

THE drawings of this object already published are very numerous, and to the same extent various and incorrect. The sources of error may easily be recognized by a practised observer as being generally due to a want of care in those adjustments of the illumination, or of the object-glass, which are fully explained in this treatise under the directions for the use of the higher-power object-glasses.

The Podura-scale is an admirable test, as it is only under the right conditions in every respect that it appears well-defined and brilliant. Nearly all the markings on the scale should appear black, but with a light median line or spot near the top; and each marking should be distinctly separate, except where it is connected longitudinally with other markings by a faint spreading line which is not perceptible with the lower powers.

There are at least five or six species of Podura which have scales of somewhat similar character to the one drawn here, but no good description of them has yet been published. The insects which have these particular scales are about $\frac{1}{10}$th of an inch long, and of a dark lead-colour; they walk slowly, but can jump a very considerable distance; and they may be found under pieces of wood or stone in outhouses which are slightly damp.

There is some difficulty in obtaining the best strongly-marked scales. An insect apparently the same as that just described is to be found almost everywhere, and will furnish scales which only differ from the right one in the markings being less brilliant and distinct. It is generally necessary to search carefully in drier parts of the locality inhabited by the insect; and under any circumstances it is advisable to make a careful comparison of specimens before being confident of having that scale which forms the best test.

The specimen here figured is a small one, but the markings are of the full size. Some further particulars of this object are given at pp. 14–17, and there are other drawings of a portion of the scale in Plate VII. figs. 1–6.

DESCRIPTION OF PLATE II.

FIRST-CLASS MICROSCOPE.

Fig. 1. Large Best, or No. 1, Stand.
- A. Joint for moving the Instrument generally, to inclined or other positions.
- B. The Body, supported by a strong limb from the joint.
- C. Milled head, for quick motion of body.
- D. Milled head, for fine adjustment of focus.
- F. Ledge of Top-stage, upon which the object is placed.
- G. Sliding-piece, to clamp the object when necessary.
- H. Milled head of Stage, for horizontal movement of object.
- I. Milled head of Stage, for vertical movement of object.
- K. The Mirror.
- L. Semicircle, in which the mirror swings.
- M. Triangular bar, upon which the mirror-fitting slides.
- N. A revolving fitting, on which the whole of the instrument above the base will turn.
- O. The draw-tube of the body, or when drawn out as in fig. 3.
- P. The Diaphragm under the stage, shown also in fig. 2.

Fig. 2.
- R. The fitting-tube of diaphragm.
- S. A short tube to receive the diaphragm, and attached by bayonet-catch to the bottom plate of stage.
- T. A cylindrical fitting, to receive all the kinds of illuminating apparatus which are required under the stage.
- U. Milled head, for movement of cylindrical fitting up or down by rack and pinion.
- W. Lengthening-arm to mirror, chiefly for supplying the means of very oblique side illumination.
- Y. Small socket, in which the forceps fit.

Fig. 3. The draw-tube of body.

(All these drawings are to a scale of one-third the true size.)

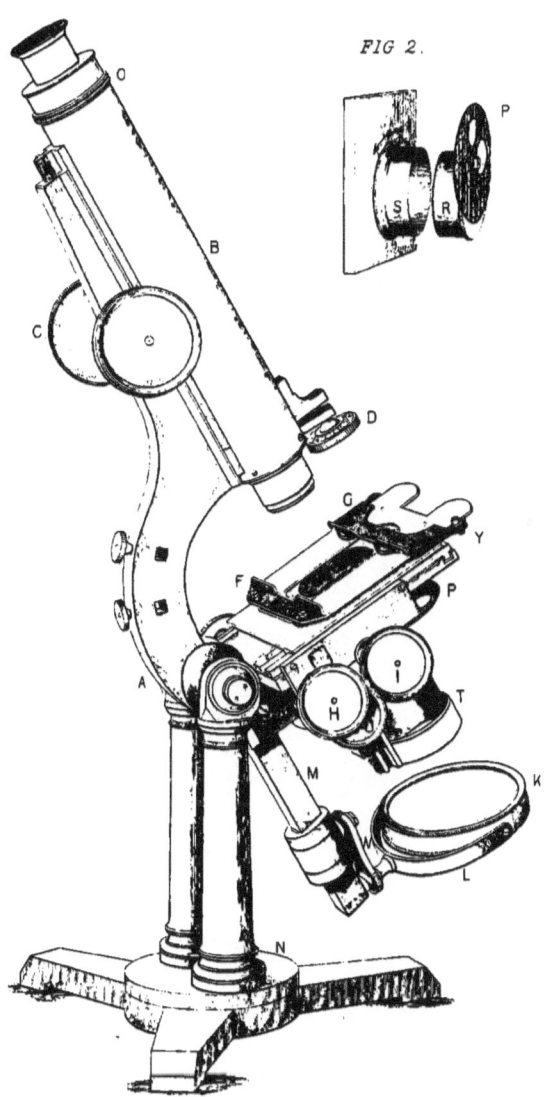

FIG. 1.

FIG 2.

⅓rd SCALE.

DESCRIPTION OF PLATE III.

FIRST-CLASS MICROSCOPE.

Small Best, or No. 2, Stand.

A. Joint for moving the Instrument generally, to inclined or other positions.
B. The Body, supported by a strong limb from the joint.
C. Milled head, for quick motion of body.
D. Milled head, for fine adjustment of focus.
F. Ledge of Top-stage, upon which the object is placed.
G. Sliding-piece, to clamp the object when necessary.
H. Milled head of Stage, for horizontal movement of object.
I. Milled head of Stage, for vertical movement of object.
K. The Mirror.
L. Semicircle, in which the mirror swings.
M. Stem tube, upon which the mirror-fitting slides.
N. A revolving fitting, on which the whole of the instrument above the base will turn.
O. The draw-tube of the body, figured when drawn out in Plate II. fig. 3.
P. The Diaphragm under the stage (for detail, see Plate II. fig. 2).
T. A cylindrical fitting, to receive all the kinds of illuminating apparatus which are required under the stage.
U. Milled head, for movement of cylindrical fitting up or down by rack and pinion.
W. Lengthening-arm to mirror, chiefly for supplying the means of very oblique side-illumination.
Y. Small socket, in which the forceps fit.

(This drawing is to a scale of one-third the true size.)

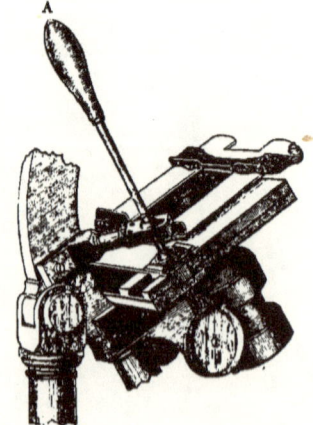

The accompanying figure shows a "lever stage" which is sometimes supplied with the First-class Instruments. It does not differ from the stage already described, so far as concerns the holding or rotation of an object; but its peculiarity consists in the arrangement for moving an object in all directions (instead of only opposite rectilinear ones) by means of a lever, which when in use is held firmly at its extremity (A) by the right hand.

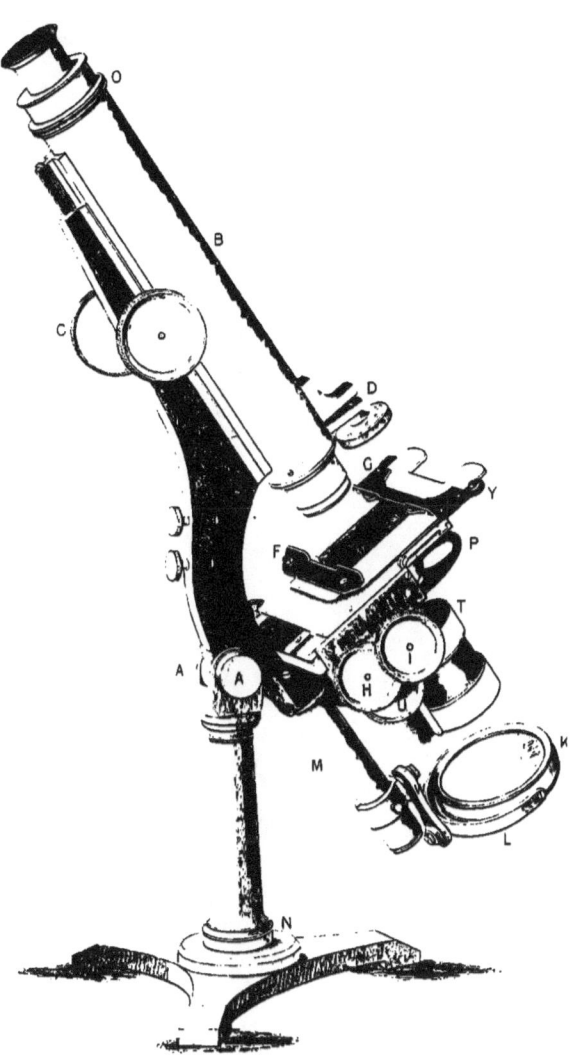

⅓rd SCALE

DESCRIPTION OF PLATE IV.

SECOND-CLASS MICROSCOPE.

The Best Student's, or No. 3, Stand.

Fig. 1. The Stand, with actions to the stage.
  A. Joint for moving the instrument generally, to inclined or other positions.
  B. The Body, supported by a limb from the stage.
  C. Milled head, for quick motion of body.
  D. Milled head, for slow motion of body.
  F. Ledge of Top-stage, upon which the object is placed.
  G. Sliding-piece, to clamp the object when necessary.
  H. Milled head of stage, for horizontal movement of object.
  I. Milled edge of stage, for vertical movement of object.
  K. The Mirror.
  L. Semicircle, in which the mirror swings.
  M. Stem tube, upon which the mirror-fitting slides.
  O. The Draw-tube of the body, figured when drawn out in Plate II. fig. 3.
  P. The Diaphragm under the stage (for detail, see Plate II. fig. 2).
  W. Lengthening-arm to mirror, chiefly for supplying the means of very oblique side-illumination.
  Y. Small socket, in which the forceps fit.

Fig. 2. Plain stage, for a Best Student's Stand.
  F. Ledge, upon which the object is placed.
  G. Sliding-piece, with spring at the end, to give a slight resistance when the object is moved sideways by the fingers, or to serve as a clamp.
  P. The Diaphragm under the stage (for further detail, see Plate II. fig. 2).
  R. A short tube, to receive the Diaphragm or any other pieces of apparatus required under the stage.
  Y. Small socket, in which the forceps fit.

(These drawings are to a scale of one-third the true size.)

FIG. 1.   FIG. 2.

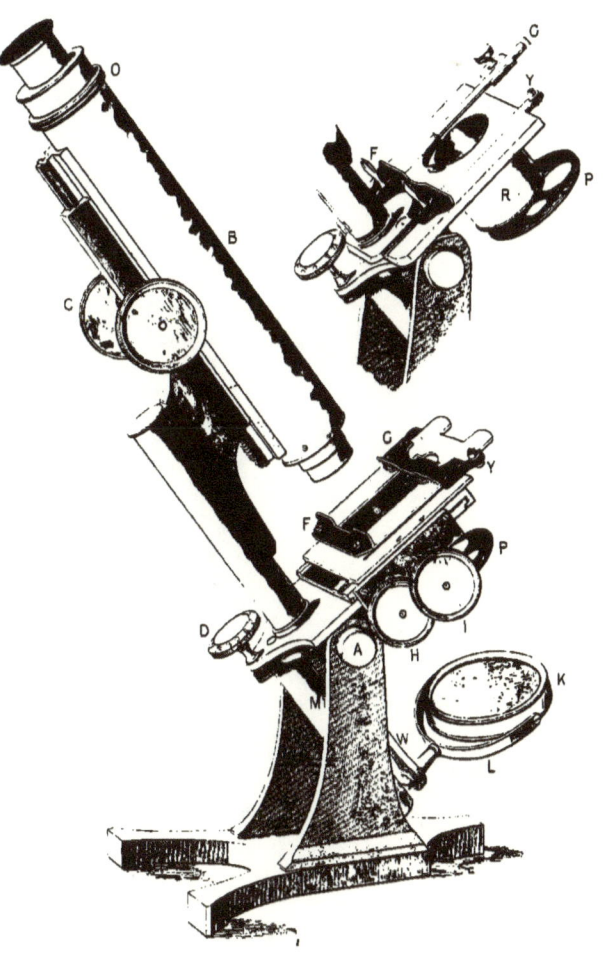

⅓rd SCALE

Description of Plate V.

Nos. 1, 2, 3. Eyepieces of different magnifying powers, No. 1 being the lowest; there are, besides these, two higher powers, viz. No. 4 and No. 5, but they do not differ in appearance from No. 3.

Fig. 4. The Erecting-glass. This is generally used in combination with the $\frac{2}{3}$rds object-glass, for the purpose of showing an object in an erect or natural position, and also for giving the great range of magnifying power of from 5 to 100 linear (for description, see p. 36).

The eight figures at the bottom of the page represent different object-glasses: the focal length is engraved on each, and the $\frac{1}{20}$th is the highest power we make; but the 2-inch is not the lowest, as we frequently supply a 3-inch.

FULL SIZE

DESCRIPTION OF PLATE VI.

Apparatus for illuminating objects from below, and two methods of measuring the apertures of object-glasses.

Fig. 1. The Achromatic Condenser, plain.
Fig. 2. The Achromatic Condenser with perforated diaphragm, a front view of which is shown in fig. 6.
Fig. 3. The Diaphragm under the stage, employed also in centering the achromatic condenser.
Fig. 4. Right-angled Prism, used instead of mirror when a more perfect reflexion is required.
Fig. 5. A small aperture of the Stage-diaphragm, as it appears in the field of view when the achromatic condenser is out of focus and not central.
Fig. 6. The Diaphragm of the Achromatic Condenser, front view (see side view, fig. 2).
Fig. 7. A small aperture of the Stage-diaphragm, as it appears in the field of view when the achromatic condenser is central and in focus.
Fig. 8. Section of Parabolic Reflector, showing the directions in which it reflects the light, for dark-field illumination.
Fig. 9. Section of Nachet's Prism, showing the directions in which it reflects the light, for oblique illumination.
Fig. 10. Nachet's Prism, as mounted for use.
Fig. 11. Amici's Prism, for oblique illumination, as mounted for use.
Fig. 12. The ordinary arrangement for measuring the aperture of object-glasses.
Fig. 13. The Parabolic Reflector, as mounted for second-class microscopes.
Fig. 14. Wenham's method of measuring apertures by a divided card.
Fig. 15. The Parabolic Reflector, as mounted for first-class microscopes.

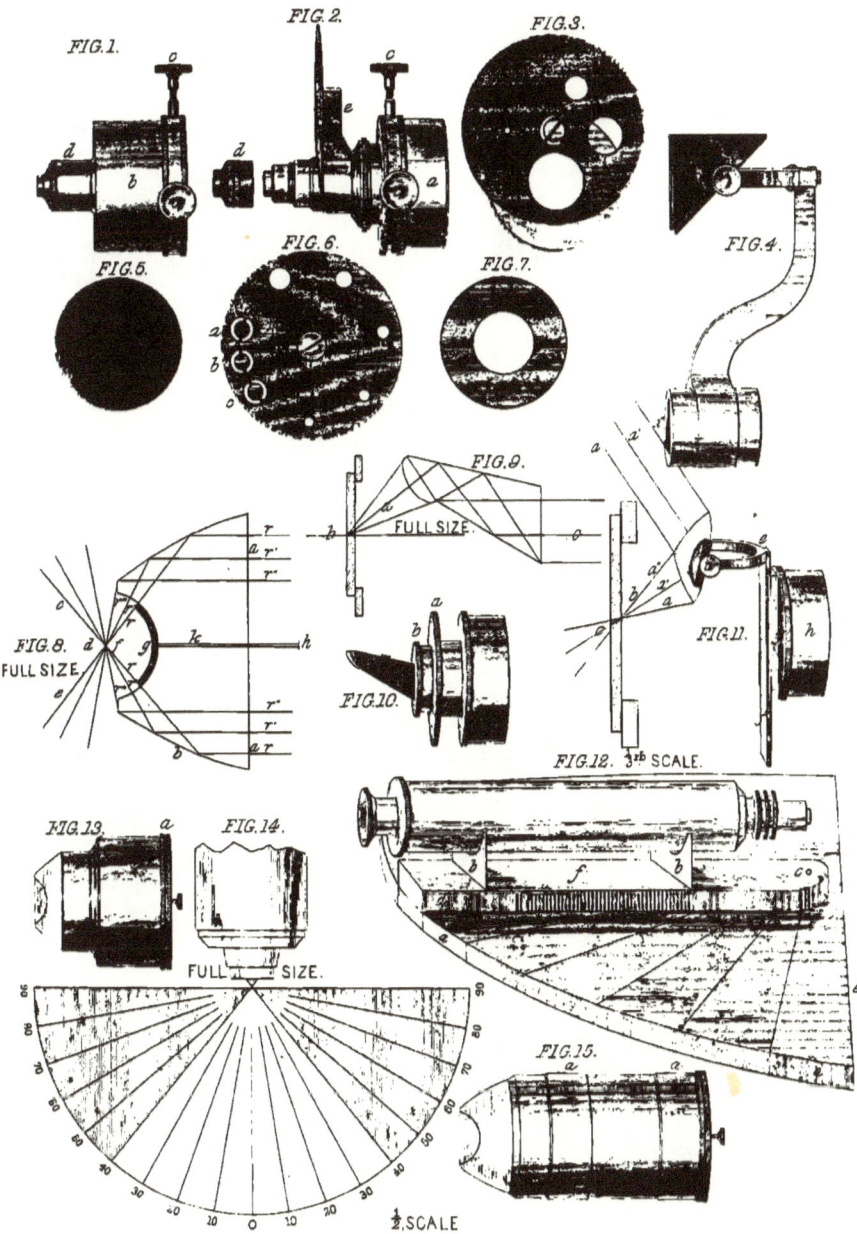

DESCRIPTION OF PLATE VII.

Fig. 1. Appearance of the Podura-scale when the adjustment of the object-glass is correct and the markings are in focus.

Fig. 2. Appearance of the Podura-scale a very little within or beyond the focus, when the adjustment of the object-glass is correct.

Fig. 3. The way in which the markings individually divide when all the adjustments are correct, and when the focus as shown in fig. 1 is altered the least possible amount either way.

Figs. 4 & 5. The two appearances on one and the other side of the best focus when the adjustment of the object-glass is incorrect.

Fig. 6. The appearance of the Podura-scale at the best focus when the adjustment of the object-glass is incorrect.

Figs. 7, 9, 10, & 12. The different directions of the lines on *Pleurosigma quadratum* under oblique illumination, in directions indicated by the arrows.

Fig. 8. Outline of *Pleurosigma quadratum*, × 400 linear.

Fig. 11. The markings on *Pleurosigma quadratum* as shown by the achromatic condenser with a large illuminating pencil.

Fig. 13. The appearance of lines on *Navicula rhomboides* when very obliquely illuminated by the Amici prism.

PLATE VII

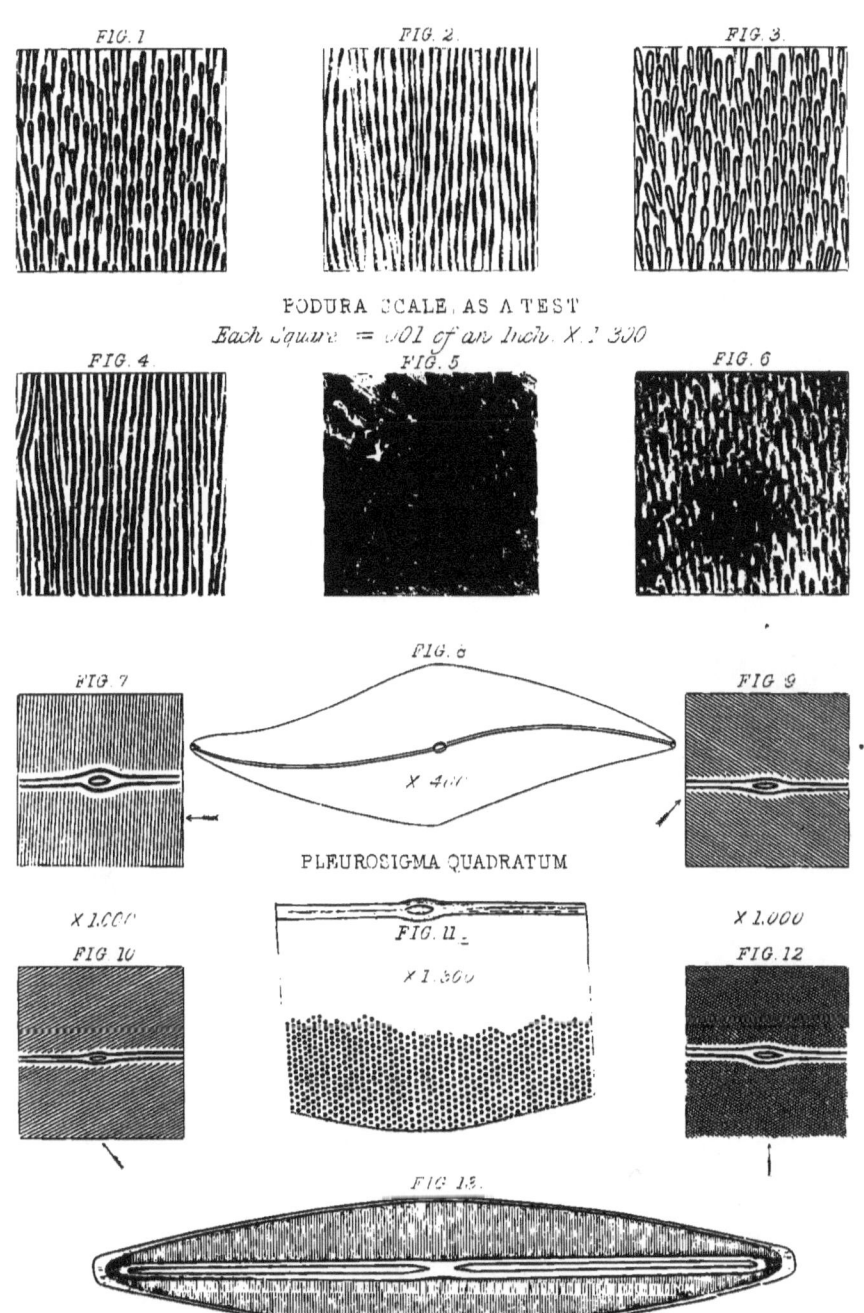

PODURA SCALE, AS A TEST
Each Square = .001 of an Inch. X 300

PLEUROSIGMA QUADRATUM

NAVICULA RHOMBOIDES, X 1.300

Description of Plate VIII.

NOBERT'S LINES.

There is but little to explain in this Plate, which is a camera-lucida drawing of the 20 bands of lines constituting the test-object known as Nobert's lines.

Under the drawing of each band is given the number of lines equivalent to one-thousandth of an inch. In the first and last bands the lines are ruled at the respective rates of 13 and 70 thousand to the inch, the other bands being intermediate, and the whole forming a beautifully graduating series.

Only the true lateral distances of the lines are intended to be given in this Plate. Their length is very considerable; and the bands follow consecutively, and not, as in this illustration, in rows one above the other.

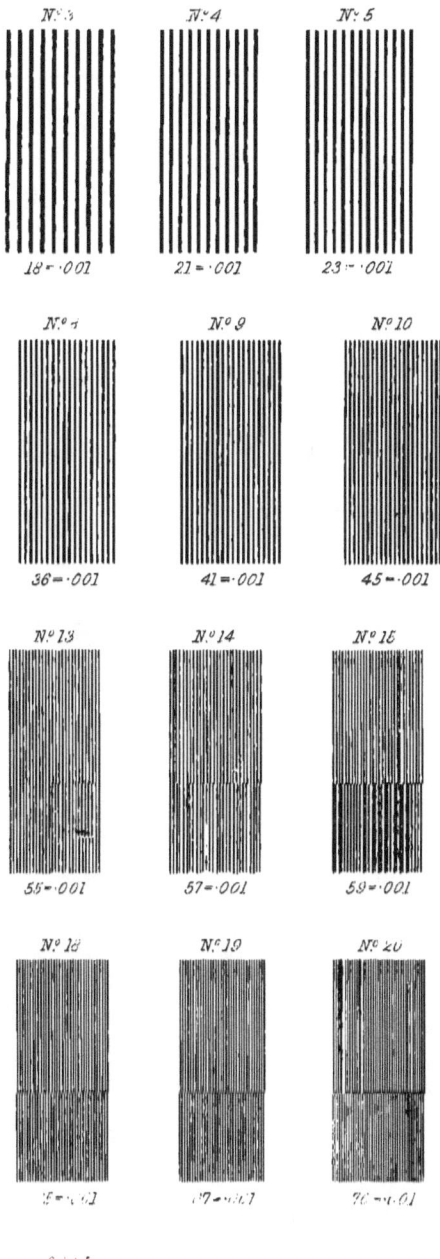

Description of Plate IX.

Fig. 1. A, B, & C represent the different appearances the markings on *Pleurosigma formosum* assume under oblique illumination in different directions. This result appears to be due to the refraction of light by more than one plane of unequal transparent structure. At D is shown an entirely different appearance, the result of central illumination with the achromatic condenser.

Fig. 2. Siliceous valve of *Pleurosigma formosum*, as seen under a low power with slightly oblique illumination.

Figs. 3, 4, 5, 6, & 7. Drawings of the cast skin from the head of the Silkworm, as seen from different points of view. These illustrations are for the purpose of showing how an object, when illuminated from above, may be examined in almost every position by means of the disk-revolver figured in Plate X. fig. 2. The object in this case was fastened to the small disk G by some gum, on the side opposite to that shown in fig. 7; and, without any alteration in this setting, the whole of the five views given here were obtained.

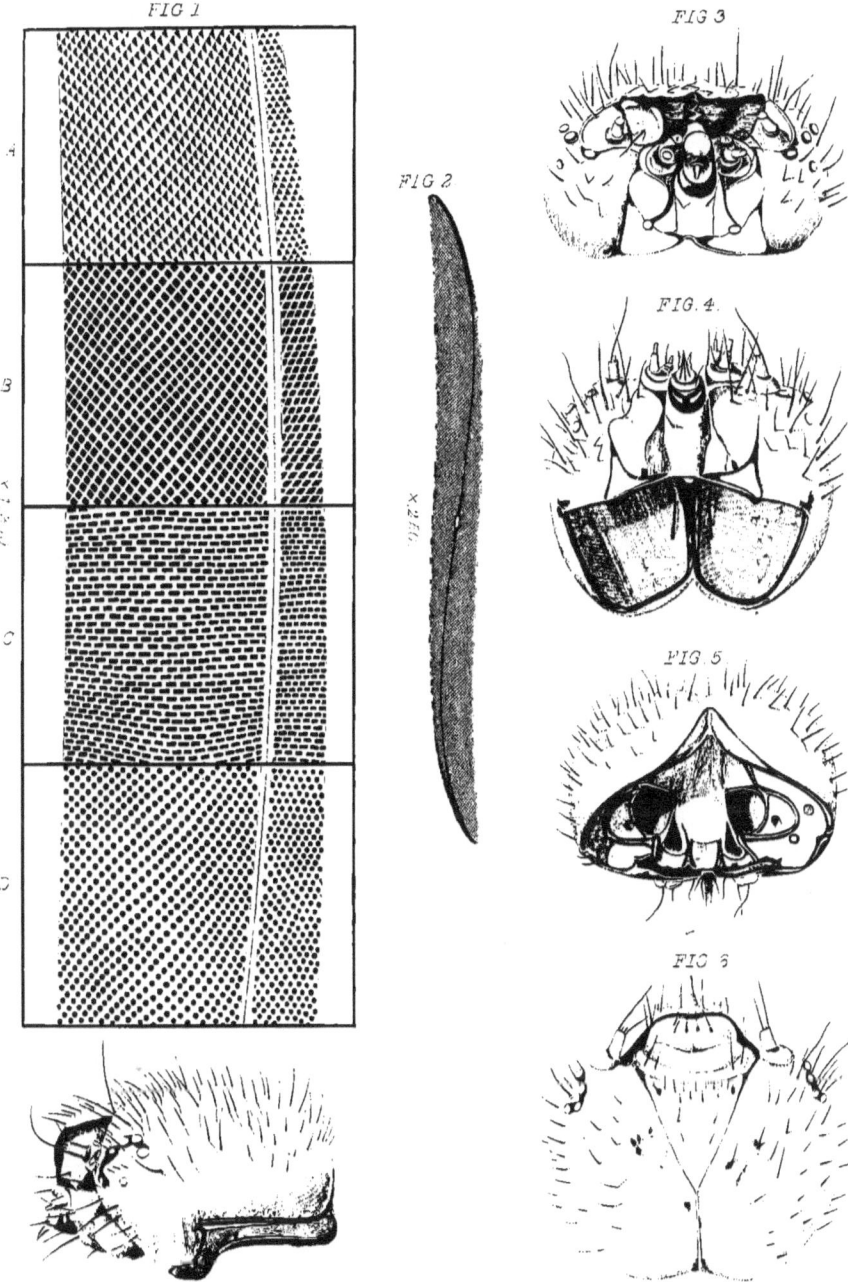

Description of Plate X.

Fig. 1. Side silver reflector, for the illumination of opaque and other objects from above.

Fig. 2. Opaque disk-revolver, an instrument for facilitating the change of position of small opaque objects.

Fig. 3. Pliers for taking hold of the small disk, G.

Fig. 4, A and B. Box for packing the small disks which fit into the opaque disk-revolver, fig. 2,—another method being shown in fig. 8.

Fig. 5. Three-pronged forceps for holding large opaque objects; they fit into a small socket on the top stage-plate.

Fig. 6. The forceps for holding small objects; the pin at A fits into a small socket on the top stage-plate.

Fig. 7. Large Bull's-eye Condenser, for concentrating the light either upon the object or the mirror.

Fig. 8. Brass plate for holding the small disks which fit into the opaque disk-revolver, fig. 2,—the other method being shown in fig. 4.

Fig. 9. Side Condensing-lens on stand, for the illumination of opaque or other objects from above.

Fig. 10. Side Condensing-lens, as adapted for first-class microscopes, for the illumination of opaque or other objects from above.

Fig. 11. Lieberkuhns for the four object-glasses specified under the figures; each of these silvered dishes fits on the front of an object-glass, and the light thrown up from the mirror below is reflected by them down upon the object.

Fig. 12. Three dark wells and a holder, for making a dark background to an object when the Lieberkuhns (fig. 11) are used.

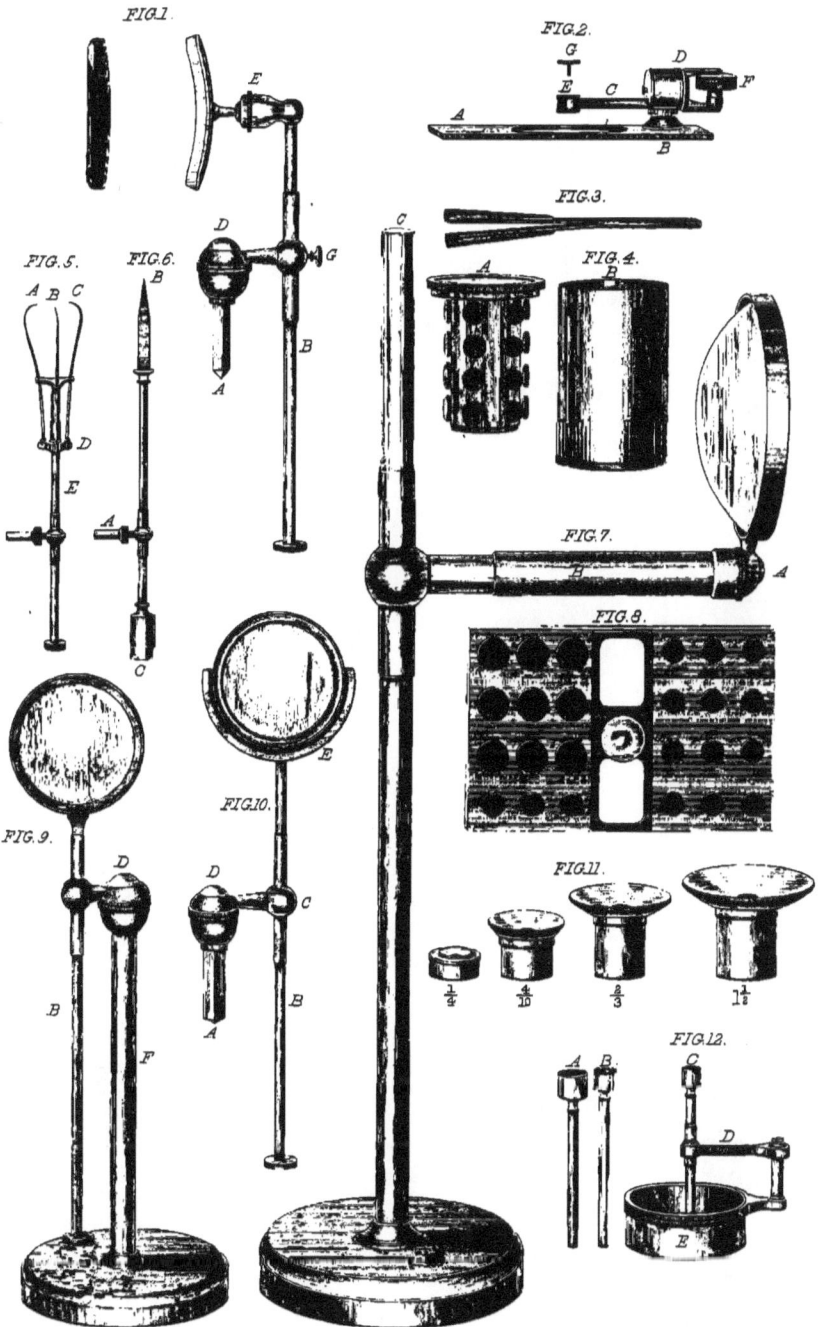

DESCRIPTION OF PLATE XI.

Fig. 1. The general appearance of coniferous wood as seen in a simple splinter. The ordinary lucifer-matches are mostly made of deal or pine, and the most beautiful specimens are easily obtained from them. Small fractured pieces of woody tissue are much superior to any sections; and in the present instance the shape of the longitudinal tubes, the form and arrangement of the circular disks or glands, together with the transverse medullary rays, form as a whole, and when under the binocular microscope, one of the most beautiful and instructive objects. It is impossible to represent their true appearance in a drawing; but we are fairly entitled to ask for a comparison between this and previous illustrations of the same subject.

Fig. 2. This illustration is intended to serve two purposes: first, the extent to which illumination from above may be carried, the magnifying power being 1300 linear, obtained by a $\frac{1}{5}$th and 3rd eyepiece; and secondly, how such an illumination may be employed in the determination of superficial structure,—A, B, and C representing the change of appearance in the markings of the Podura-scale when they are placed in different directions to the light. (This subject is treated of in detail at page 29.)

PLATE XI.

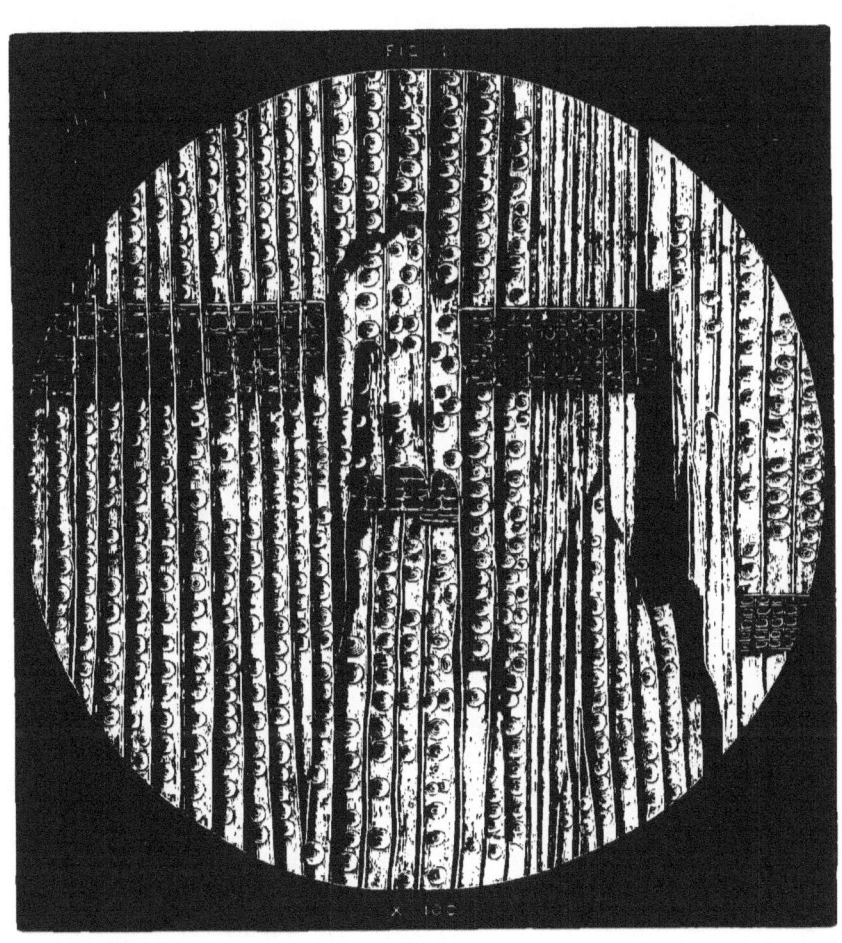

FIG. 2

A B C

R. Beck, del.   × 1300.

Description of Plate XII.

Fig. 1. Tarsus of *Tegenaria atrica* (a spider very common in outhouses) as seen by Lieberkuhn illumination. It is an interesting and beautiful object, from the variety of hairs with which it is studded: besides those of the upper and under sides being very different in general shape, there is a distinct group round the claws, a few scattered branching hairs, others again which approach to spines, and lastly, and perhaps the most interesting of all, some very delicate hairs which rise more or less at right angles from the upper surface of the joint, and during life wave about from a ball-and-socket root when there is the least motion in the air, and are no doubt intimately connected in some way with sensation. The larger figures of the hairs show that they also are all covered with other minute short hairs, the distinct separation of which forms a very good test for an object-glass.

Figs. 2 & 4. Part of a Pigeon's feather, showing the arrangement by which the barbs are attached to each other. The top and bottom figures are respectively the upper and under surfaces of the vane of the feather, whilst fig. 3 is a section in the direction of the letters a, b, and shows the barbules (c) and the barbulettes (e).

PLATE XII.

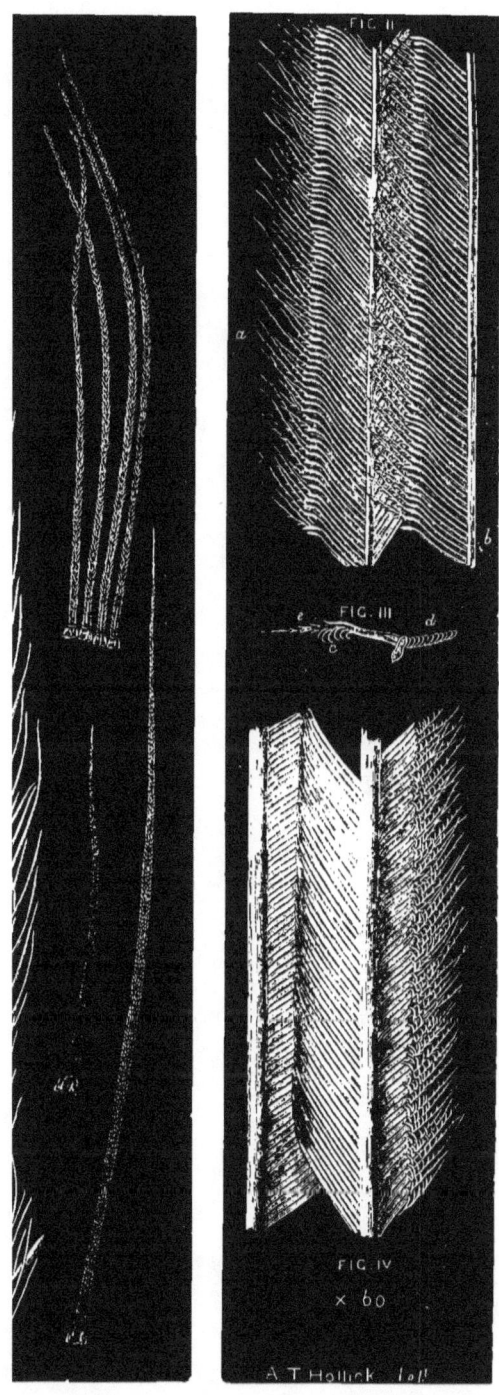

DESCRIPTION OF PLATE XIII.

THE *ARACHNOIDISCUS JAPONICUS.*

THIS illustration is given to show the result that can be obtained with a $\frac{1}{4}$-inch object-glass and Lieberkuhn illumination.

The drawings have been made from specimens most kindly lent us by Mr. Deane, of Clapham, who was the first to draw the attention of microscopists to this diatom in its natural position, having found it in considerable abundance on some seaweed used in Japan for soups.

Our Plate, however, does not represent specimens from this locality, but from a marine plant of Mauritius, given to Mr. Deane by Professor Harvey, of Dublin.

The three figures in the Plate, although drawn from valves of different sizes, serve just as well to explain the structure of this diatom. The bottom right-hand figure shows the complete form, two siliceous valves being joined by a connecting membrane; but the process of self-division has commenced, as indicated by the narrow central light band. The other figure at the bottom gives the appearance of the external surface of the valve, whilst the more striking structure of the internal surface is represented in the larger figure above.

PLATE XIII.

X. 550
R. Beck del.

Description of Plate XIV.

This Plate is intended to show the effect produced by "dark-field illumination" on some of the Polycystina found in an extensive fossil deposit in the island of Barbadoes. Of the true character of these beautiful microscopic objects, which are closely allied to the Foraminifera, there is but little known; they were discovered by Professor Ehrenberg, and by him have been most carefully classified. There is every reason to suppose that most of the specimens in the mounted slides are more or less mutilated; this, however, does not detract from their remarkable beauty as microscopic objects, nor from their value as illustrating the advantages of a peculiar illumination, for which purpose they are introduced here.

The following are the names of Figs. 2, 3, and 4. Figs. 1 and 2 we are unable to identify with any illustrations that have been published.

Fig. 1.
Fig. 2. *Haliomma Humboldtii.*
Fig. 3. *Astromma Aristotelis.*
Fig. 4. *Lychnocanium lucerna.*
Fig. 5.

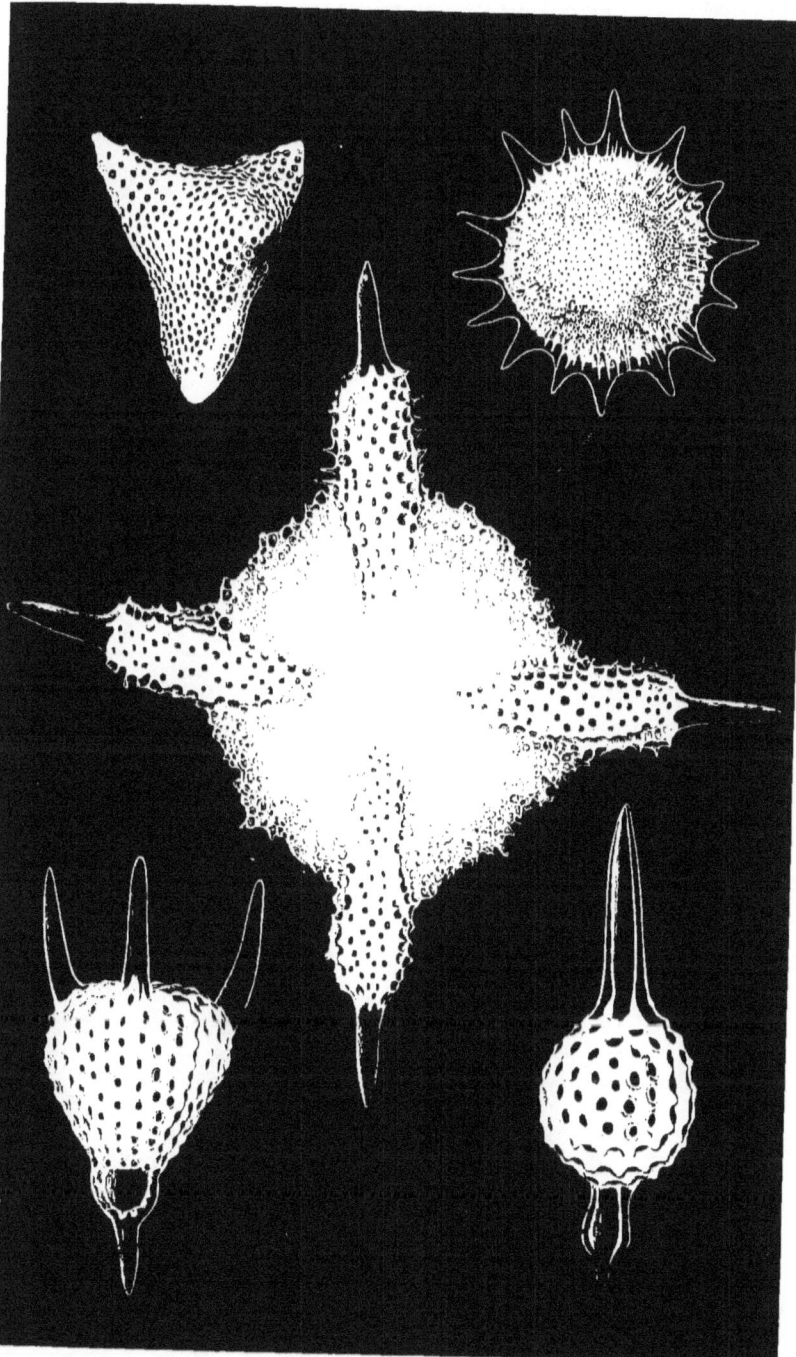

DESCRIPTION OF PLATE XV.

THESE illustrations are to explain the use and capabilities of the Erecting-glass, which may be employed with great advantage when objects of a large size have to be examined under low powers of from 5 to 100 linear; and with it the image of the object is erect, not reversed, which considerably helps in any manipulation or dissection of the object.

Fig. 1. The new halfpenny coin of the realm, magnified only 5 times linear, by employing the erecting-glass with the ⅔rds.

Figs. 2 & 3. The two sides of a halfpenny, the full size. These figures, when compared with fig. 1, convey a good idea of linear magnifying power.

Fig. 4. The foot only of the figure of Britannia under a magnifying power increased to 25 diameters, obtained by pulling out the draw-tube of the body; and by the same process the range of power may be extended to 100 diameters, but this object then becomes quite unsuitable as an illustration.

PLATE XV

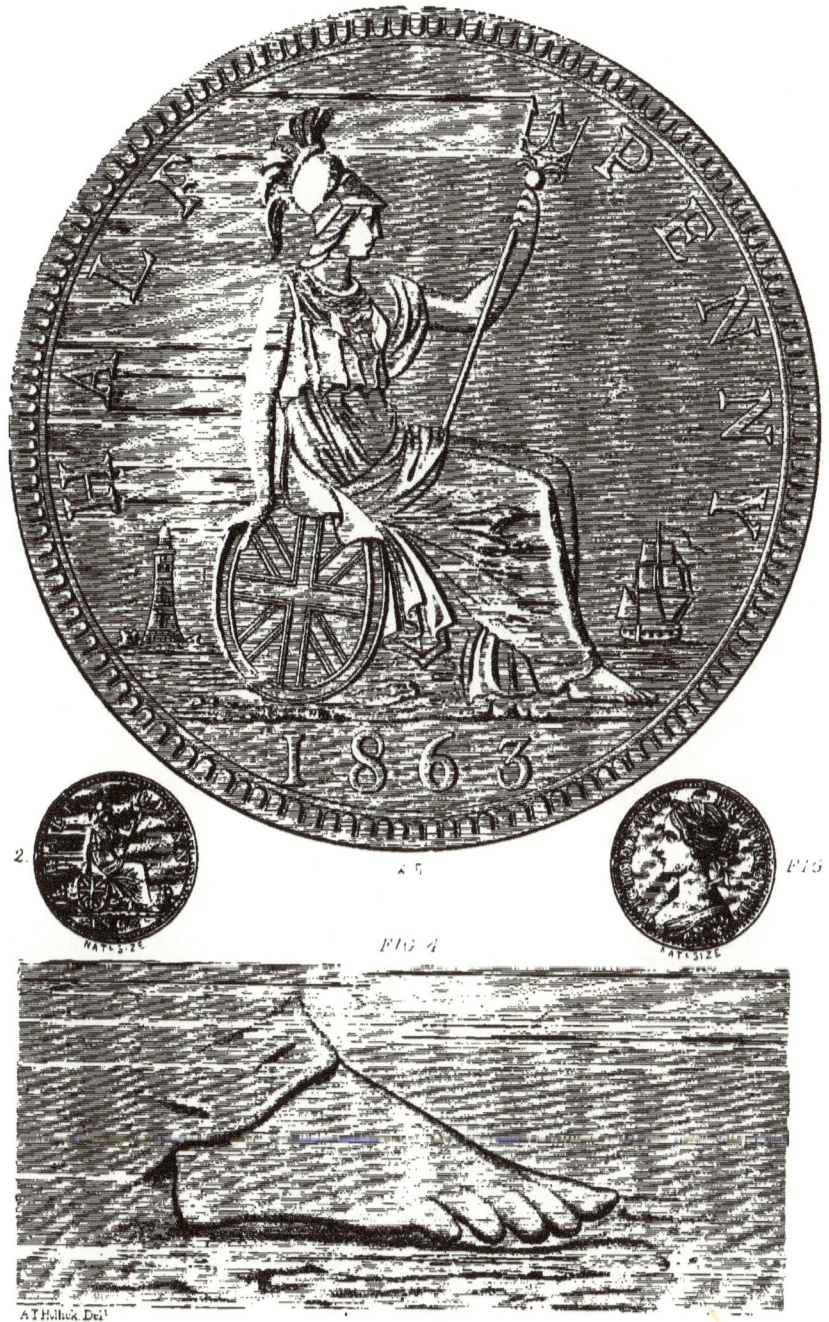

Description of Plate XVI.

Fig. 1. The short tube, fitting by a bayonet-catch to the under plate of the stage.
Fig. 2. The ordinary polarizer of Nicol's prism.
Fig. 3. The extra-large polarizer of Nicol's prism.
Fig. 4. The analyzer of Nicol's prism.
Fig. 5. Tourmaline mounted as an analyzer.
Fig. 6. The selenite plate.
Fig. 7. The ring to hold the selenite plate in its fitting, fig. 8.
Fig. 8. The fitting for the selenite plate, fig. 6.
Figs. 9, 10, 11. Darker's three retarding-films of selenite.
Figs. 12, 13. Two of Darker's retarding-films when placed at right angles.
Fig. 14. Darker's selenite stage.
Fig. 15. The analyzer of Nicol's prism when its cap and its fitting to the eyepiece are removed to suit it for either of the adapters, figs. 19 or 20.
Fig. 16. Darker's three retarding-films, fitted to rotating cells of three arms, which, when in use, fit on the cylindrical fitting under the stage, as shown in fig. 22.
Fig. 17. Selenite mounted in plain brass plate.
Fig. 18. Selenite mounted between two slips of glass.
Fig. 19. An adapter which screws into a stop at the bottom of the draw-tube to receive the analyzer, fig. 15.
Fig. 20. An adapter which screws on the nosepiece of the microscope to receive the analyzer, fig. 15.
Fig. 21. A polarizer of polished black glass, fitting on the rim of the mirror.
Fig. 22. The Achromatic Condenser combined with a polarizer, and Darker's series of selenites, to increase the brilliancy of the colours under high powers.
Fig. 23. A bundle of thin glass as a polarizer.
Figs. 24, 25, 26. Two double-image prisms and plate of selenite, for experiments with double refraction.
Fig. 27. A brass plate with three small holes for use with double-image prisms.
Fig. 28. A section of a crystal as mounted to show rings.

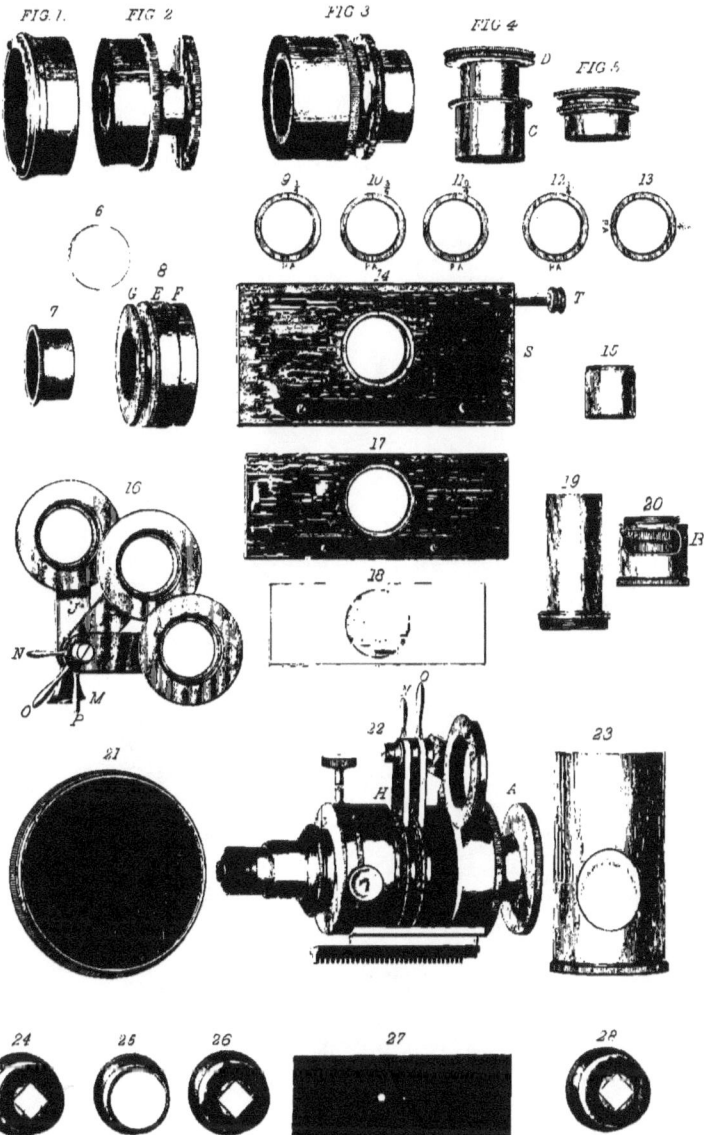

DESCRIPTION OF PLATE XVII.

OBJECTS SEEN UNDER POLARIZED LIGHT.

Fig. 1. A crystal of the sulphate of copper and magnesia as it appears when the Nicol's prisms only are used.

Fig. 2. The same object, showing the change produced by the addition of a selenite plate.

Fig. 3. An oblique section of Rhinoceros-horn as seen under polarized light produced by Nicol's prisms only.

Fig. 4. A section of the tendon of the Ostrich under polarized light produced by Nicol's prisms only.

Figs. 5 & 6. Crystallized salicine (an alkaloid from the bark of the willow) under polarized light produced by Nicol's prisms only. The two drawings show the change produced by one quarter of a revolution of one of the prisms.

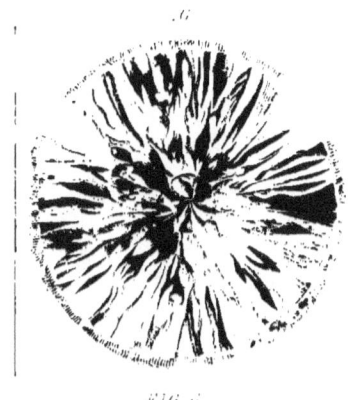

FIG. 1.

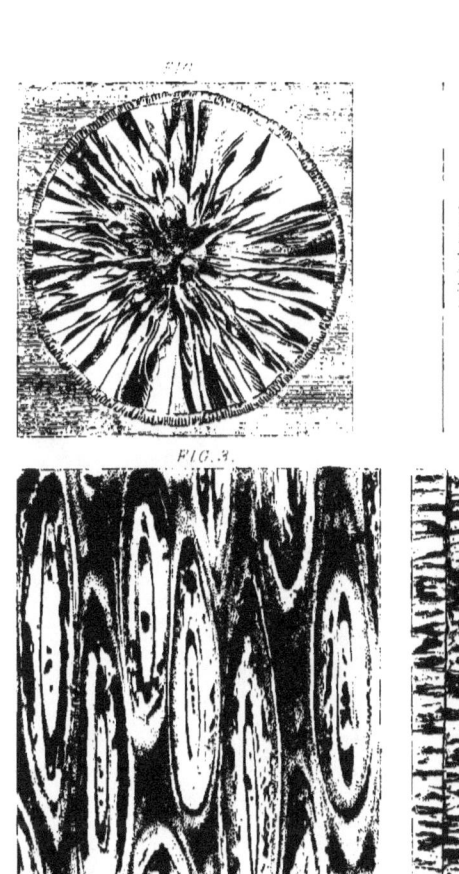

FIG. 3.

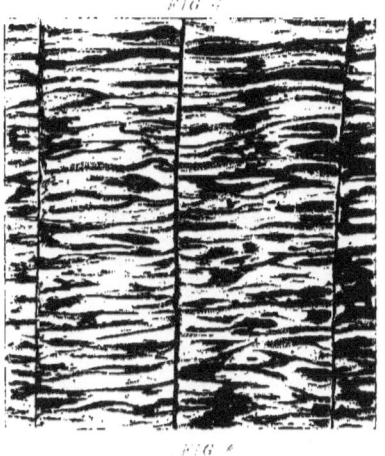

FIG. 2.

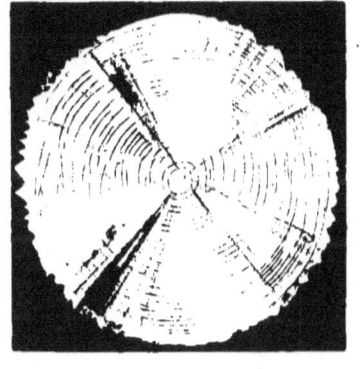

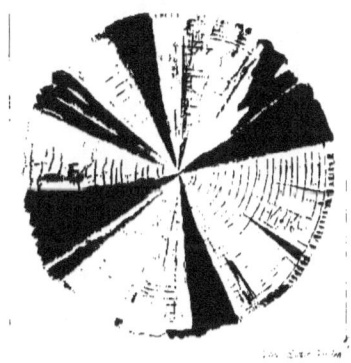

Description of Plate XVIII.

ILLUSTRATIONS OF EXPERIMENTS WITH DOUBLE-IMAGE PRISMS.

Fig. 1. The appearance of three small holes when a double-image prism is placed over the eyepiece.

Fig. 2. The same as fig. 1, with the addition of a polarizer and an interposed plate of selenite. Where the larger images overlap, the complementary tints form white light.

Fig. 3. The change that takes place in the double image, at four equal points, in one revolution of the polarizer.

Fig. 4. The same experiment as that shown in fig. 3, but with the interposition of a plate of selenite.

Fig. 5. The appearances of a small hole, without a polarizer, but with two double-refracting prisms placed over the eyepiece; and the changes that take place when one of the prisms is moved round to four equal points in one revolution.

Fig. 6. The same experiment as fig. 5 repeated, with the addition of a polarizer and interposed plate of selenite.

Fig. 7. A diagram to show when the Nicol's prism is adjusted with its acute angles parallel with the sides of the stage.

Fig. 8. A diagram to show the natural flaws or veins in the selenite plate, and the position in which the greatest amount of depolarization may be obtained.

Fig. 9. A diagram to show when the Nicol's prism is turned 45 degrees from the position shown in fig. 7, and when no depolarization will take place.

Fig. 10. The black cross and coloured rings produced by a piece of calc-spar when its surfaces are cut perpendicular to the axis of the crystal, and when placed under polarized light, by fitting over the cap of the eyepiece of the microscope with an analyzer above.

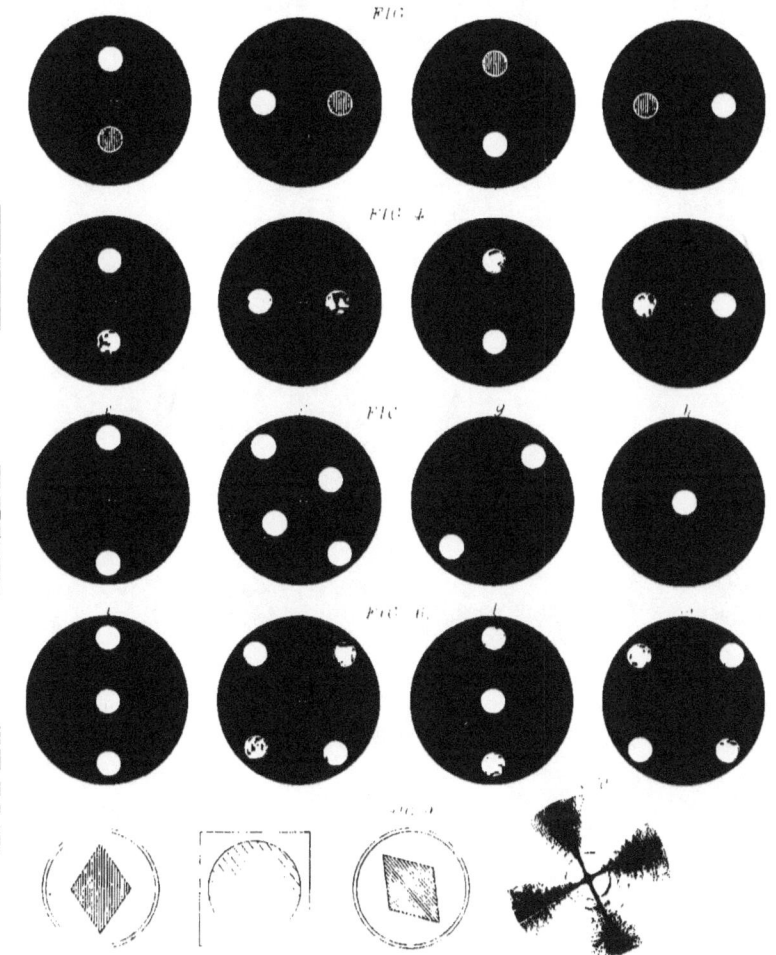

DESCRIPTION OF PLATE XIX.

STRUCTURE OF THE SCALES OF *LEPISMA SACCHARINA*.

Fig. 1 (*a* and *b*). The different appearances, on a small scale, of *Lepisma saccharina* when the superficial corrugations cross at different angles.

Fig. 2 (*c*). The appearance resulting from the superposition of two scales.

Fig. 3. One of the more common scales of *Lepisma saccharina* under a magnifying power of 650 linear.

Fig. 4. Parts of a scale in which the appearances have been altered, by the structure on opposite sides being obliterated by moisture.

PLATE XX.

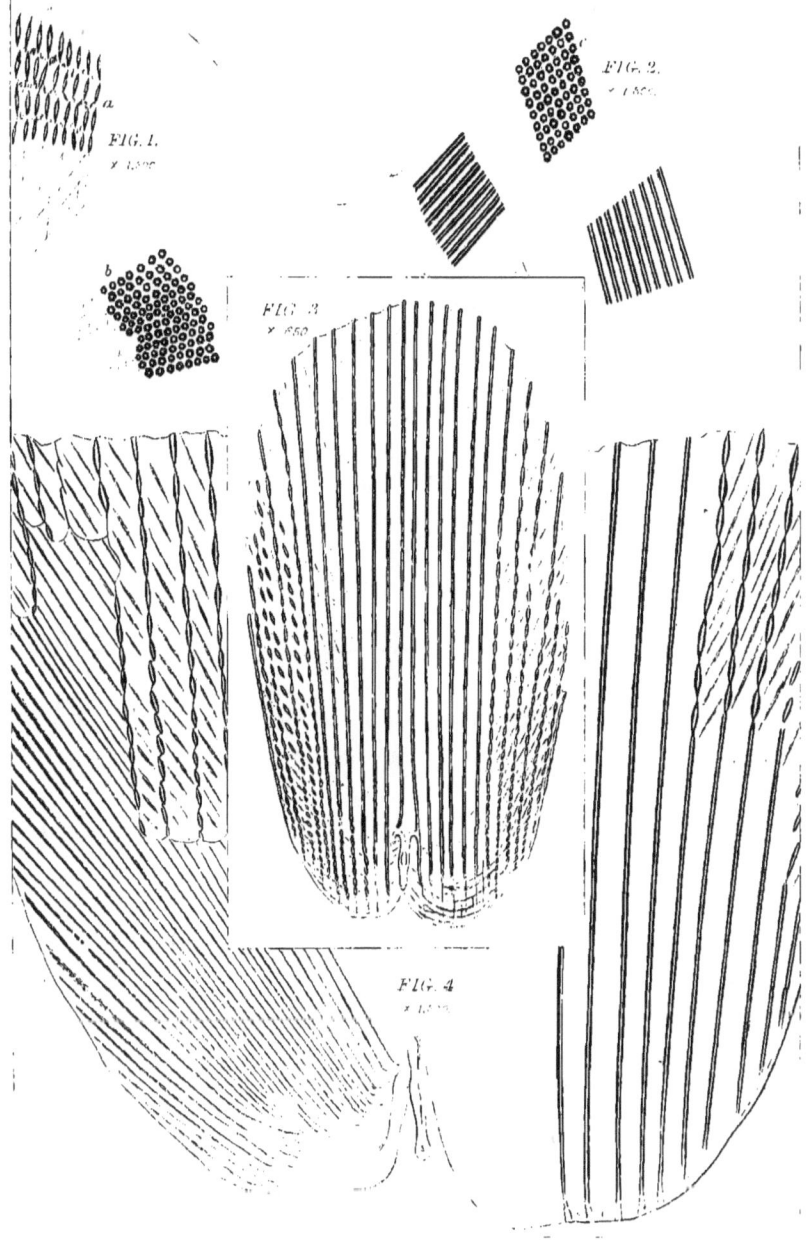

FIG. 1.
FIG. 2.
FIG. 3.
FIG. 4.

DESCRIPTION OF PLATE XX.

Fig. 1. The body and part of the limb of one of the ordinary microscope-stands, with an additional tube, forming Wenham's Binocular Microscope. This addition does not interfere with the ordinary use of the single body, and any of the microscope-stands as yet figured will admit of the alteration.
- B. The additional body-tube.
- C. The original body-tube.
- D & E. Draw-tubes.
- I. The part of the nosepiece where the prism-box is inserted.
- K. The milled head, connected with a pinion and racks, by which the draw-tubes D and E may be adjusted for eyes of different distances.

Fig. 2. An adapter to receive the analyzer of the polarizing apparatus, so that polarized light may be employed with the binocular body.

Fig. 3. The fitting for the small prism, which reflects one-half of the rays passing through the object-glass into the additional tube of the binocular body.
- F. A small catch for stopping the prism-box when it is drawn back so as to allow the whole of the rays from the object-glass to pass into the straight body. This catch must be pressed back when the prism-box has to be removed.

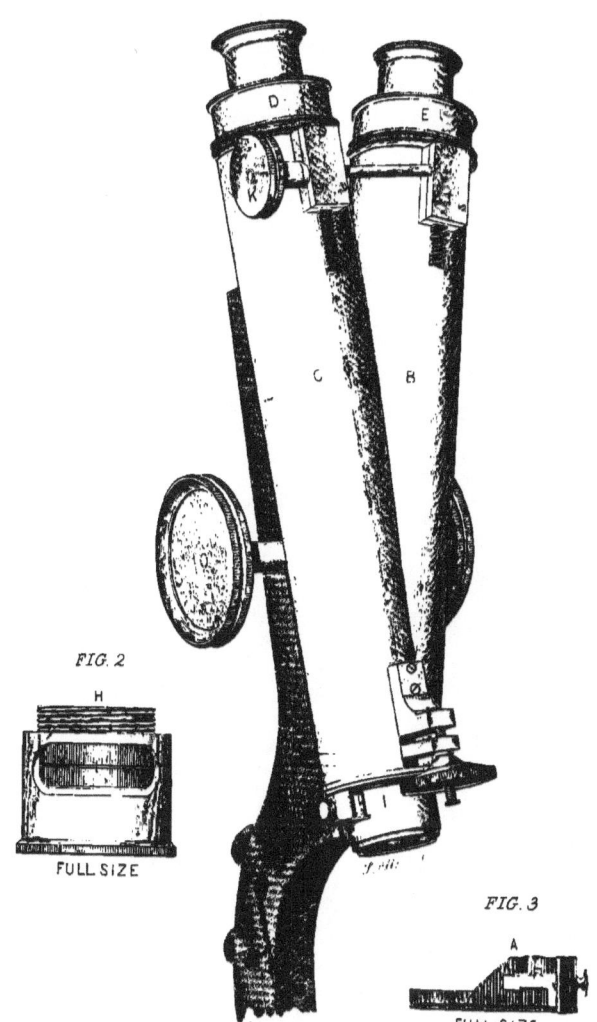

FIG. 2

FULL SIZE

½ SCALE

FIG. 3

FULL SIZE

DESCRIPTION OF PLATE XXI.

LIVE-BOXES, COMPRESSORS, &c.

Fig. 1. Small live-box.
Fig. 2. Glass trough, front view.
Fig. 3. Glass trough, end view.
Fig. 4. Large live-box, with the cap lifted from lower part.
Fig. 5. Glass plate with ledge, and thin glass cover.
Fig. 6. Three glass tubes for catching animalcules.
Fig. 7. Wenham's Compressor, front view.
Fig. 8. Wenham's Compressor, side view.
Fig. 9. Screw live-box, front view.
Fig. 10. Screw live-box, side view.
Fig. 11. Parallel plate compressor when the plates are separated.
Fig. 12. Parallel plate compressor when the plates are close together.
Fig. 13. Lever compressor, front view.
Fig. 14. Lever compressor, side view.
Fig. 15. The arrangement of the two pieces of thin glass in the two compressors, figs. 11 & 17.
Fig. 16. Counter cell of the compressor, fig. 17.
Fig. 17. The reversible cell compressor.
Fig. 18. The cell of the compressor, fig. 17.
Fig. 19. The frog plate.

FIG. 1.

FIG. 2.

FIG. 3.

FIG. 4.

FIG. 5.

FIG. 6.

FIG. 7.

FIG. 8.

FIG. 9.

FIG. 10.

FIG. 11.

FIG. 12.

FIG. 13.

FIG. 14.

FIG. 15.

FIG. 16.

FIG. 17.

FIG. 19.

½ SCALE.

FIG. 18.

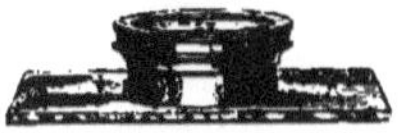

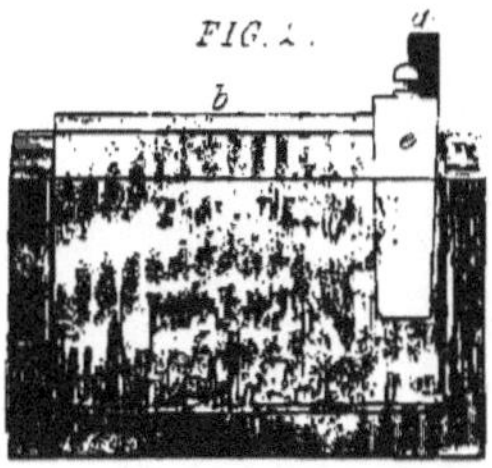

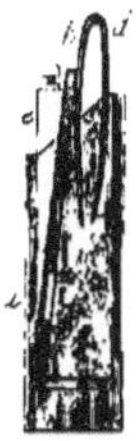

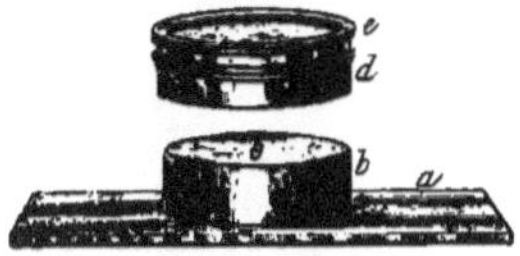

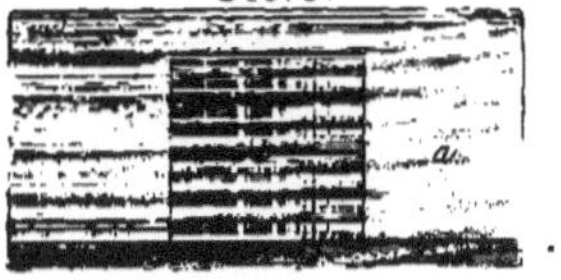

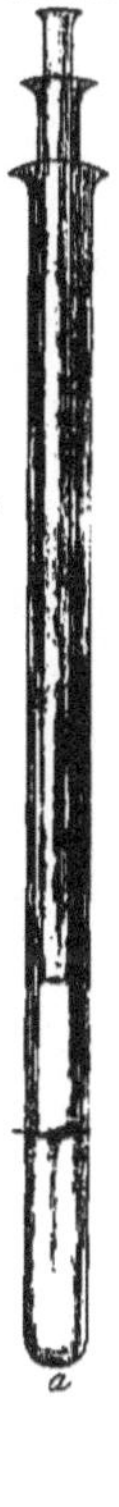

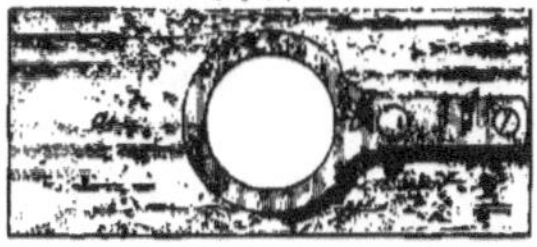

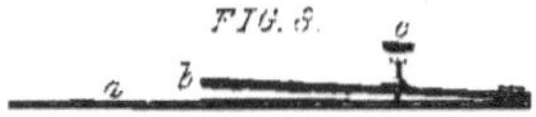

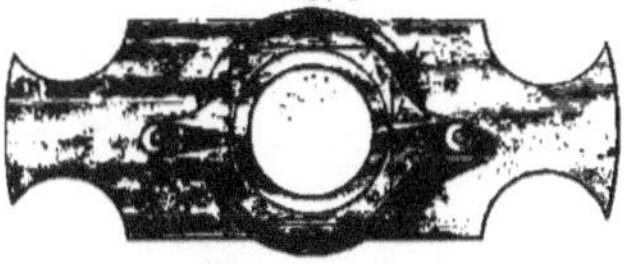

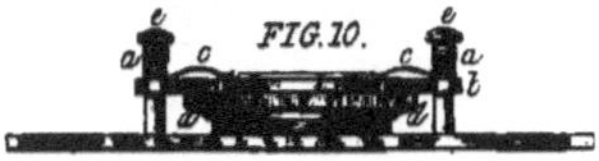

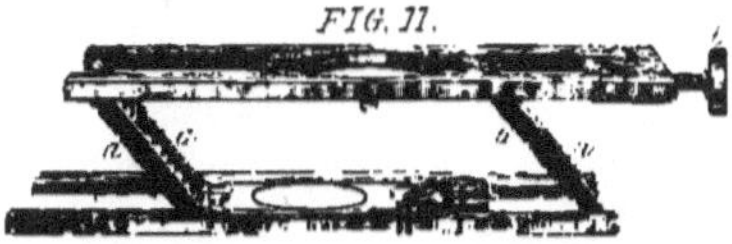

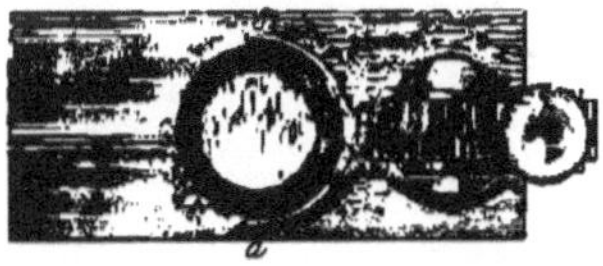

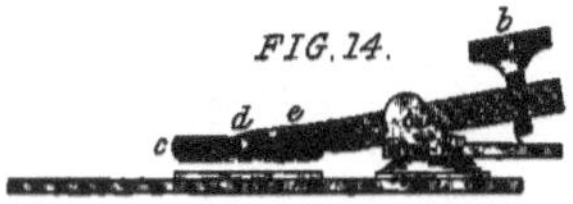

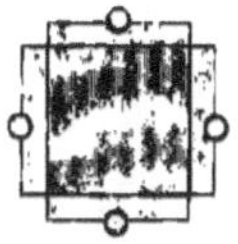

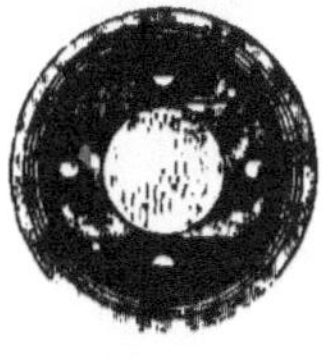

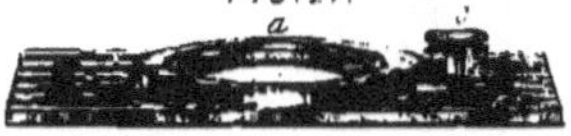

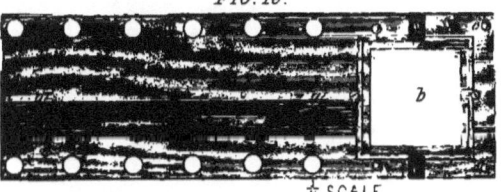

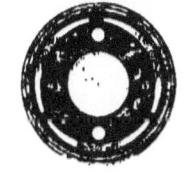

DESCRIPTION OF PLATE XXII.

MICROMETERS, CAMERA LUCIDA, &c.

Fig. 1. No. 2 Eyepiece, with the micrometer in position. The cap of the eyepiece is here drawn apart, to show how the top lens may be adjusted at *a*.
Fig. 2. The Eyepiece Micrometer, front view.
Fig. 3. The Stage Micrometer, as mounted in brass.
Fig. 4. The Stage Micrometer, mounted in card.
Fig. 5. The lines of the eyepiece and stage micrometers, as they appear in the field of view.
Fig. 6. The Camera Lucida, as seen from above.
Fig. 7. The Camera Lucida, side view.
Fig. 8. A drawing to scale, showing the way to draw an object in the microscope by means of the Camera Lucida.
Fig. 9. The top view of an eyepiece, showing the small arc at *a*, by which Quekett's Indicator may be turned in or out of the field of view.
Fig. 10. Quekett's Indicator, as it appears when in the field of view.
Fig. 11. A sketch, made by the Camera Lucida, of the stellate tissue of a rush; the right-hand portion is more or less touched up, but that on the left is exactly as traced by aid of the camera.
Fig. 12. Leeson's Goniometer.
Fig. 13. A quadruple nosepiece, for the attachment of four object-glasses to the microscope at once.
Fig. 14. A double nosepiece, for the attachment of two object-glasses to the microscope at once.

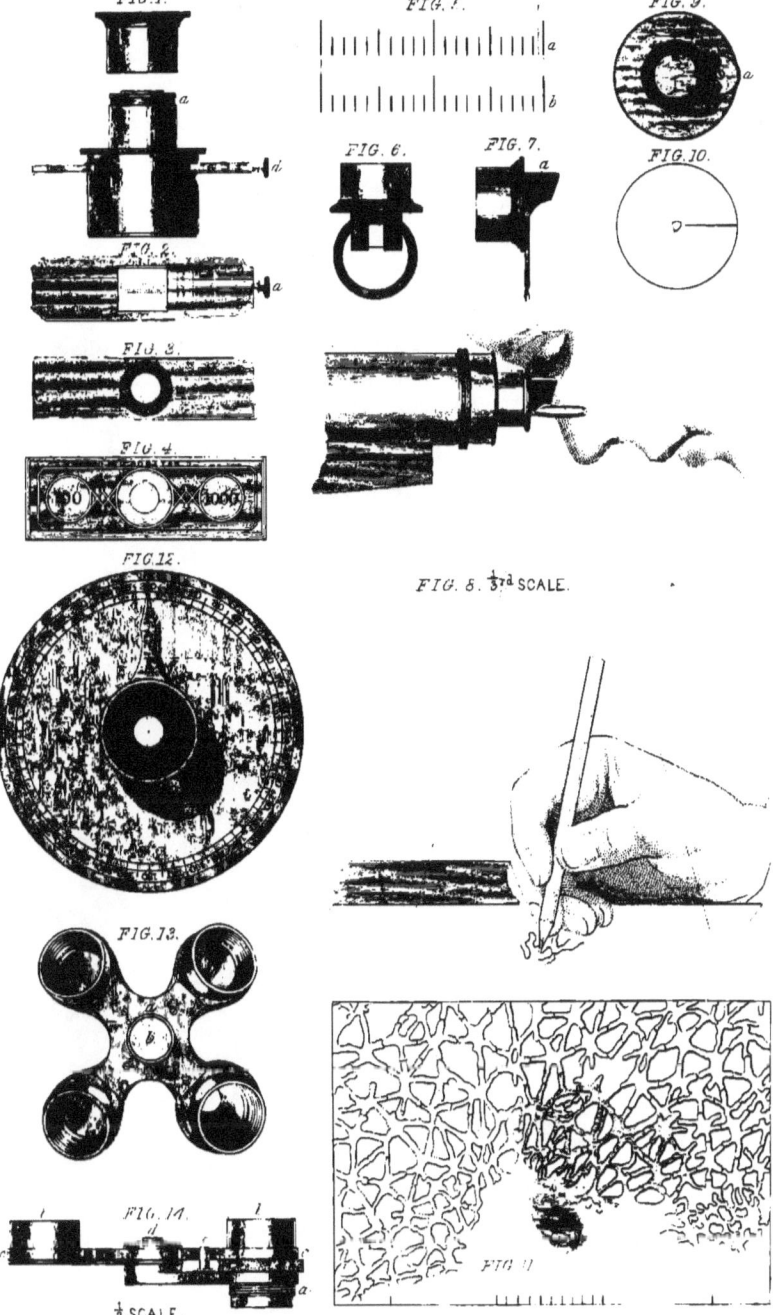

DESCRIPTION OF PLATE XXIII.

LAMPS AND REVOLVING TABLE FOR THE MICROSCOPE.

Fig. 1. Cambridge reading-lamp for burning oil.
Fig. 2. Best Belmontine lamp, with circular wick.
Fig. 3. Cheaper Belmontine lamp, with flat wick.
Fig. 4. Gas-lamp for use with flexible tube.
Fig. 5. An engraving to show the use of the revolving microscope-table. Only two sitters are represented in the Plate; but three or four persons may sit round without inconvenience.

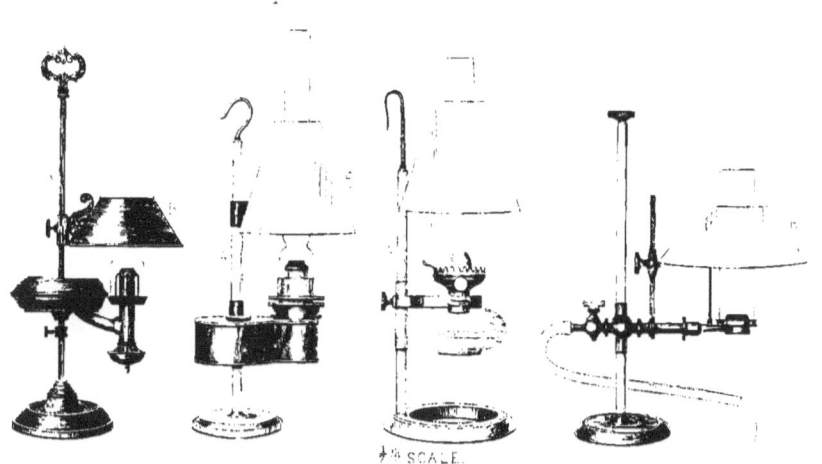

DESCRIPTION OF PLATE XXIV.

OBJECTS AS SEEN UNDER THE $\frac{1}{20}$TH OBJECT-GLASS MAGNIFYING 900 LINEAR.

Fig. 1. The thorax, legs, and parts of head, as seen on the under side, of *Demodex folliculorum*, a parasite found in the follicles of the human skin, more especially about the nose.

A & B. Moveable organs, which are probably palpi; but the correct determination of the various parts of this parasite is very difficult, on account of its transparency, which confuses the upper and under portions, whilst the denser parts of its structure refract the light and falsify the appearances of many of the features.

Figs. 2 & 3. Front and profile views of the stinging-hairs from the stem of the common nettle (*Urtica dioica*).

Fig. 4. A stinging-hair similar to those in the preceding figures, but with the bulbous extremity broken off by being touched: in this way a very sharp point is provided, which is admirably adapted for puncturing; and an aperture being made at the same time, the fluid escapes from the interior of the hair and enters the wound.

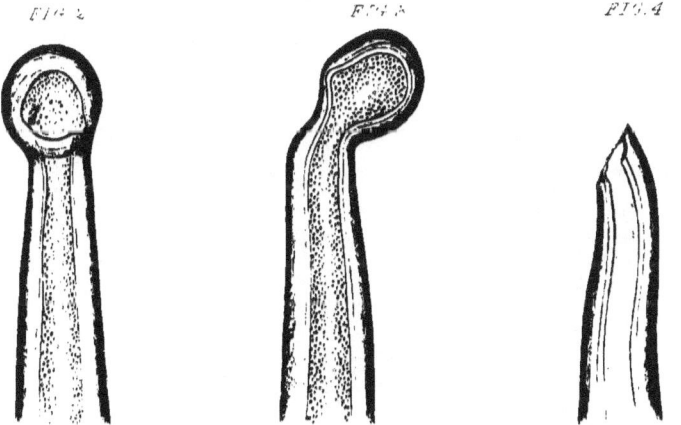

FIG. 1. 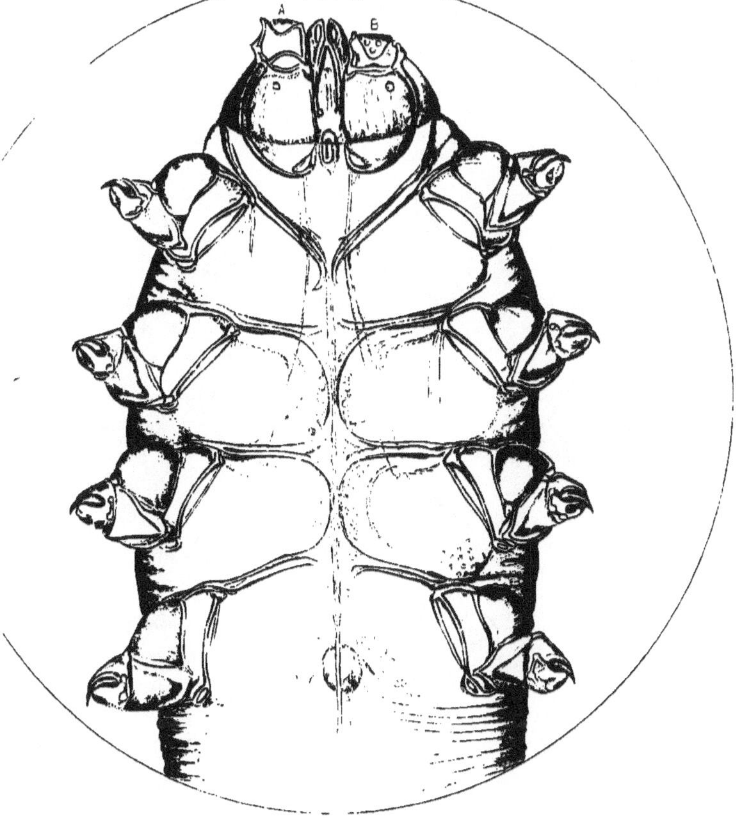
FIG. 2. FIG. 3. FIG. 4.

DESCRIPTION OF PLATE XXV.

THE BEST UPRIGHT CASE FOR THE LARGE BEST MICROSCOPE.

THIS Plate shows the way in which the Large Best Binocular Microscope, together with the most complete apparatus, is packed in an upright case. The extremities of the tripod base are let into a board at the bottom, to facilitate the sliding of the instrument either in or out, and also to confine it to one fixed position; the eyepiece ends are also secured by two grooves, the central one having a sliding dovetail block which fills up the intervening space between the eyepiece and the door.

The Bull's-eye Condenser is fastened by various packings on the back of the case, and the long draw-tube fits into two blocks on the left, the remaining apparatus being packed in two boxes which slide on either side of the Microscope-stand. (The interiors of these boxes are shown in the next Plate.) By this arrangement, when the door is closed, the whole instrument is securely packed for any kind of ordinary travelling.

PLATE XXV.

⅓rd scale.

DESCRIPTION OF PLATE XXVI.

THE TWO BOXES OF APPARATUS BELONGING TO A COMPLETE LARGE BEST MICROSCOPE.

THERE is but little explanation required for this Plate, which shows the various ways in which the different object-glasses, eyepieces, and other apparatus are packed in the two boxes, which in the preceding Plate are shown as packed on either side of the Microscope-stand.

Each separate piece of apparatus is held in these cases, when they are closed, by a block on the lid; so that all are secure from any injury by displacement when the cases are turned over or are shaken.

This Plate may also be of some service to a beginner, who may occasionally find some difficulty in replacing the apparatus; for, unless each piece is in its proper place, the cases cannot be closed without some strain or injury.

PLATE XXVI.

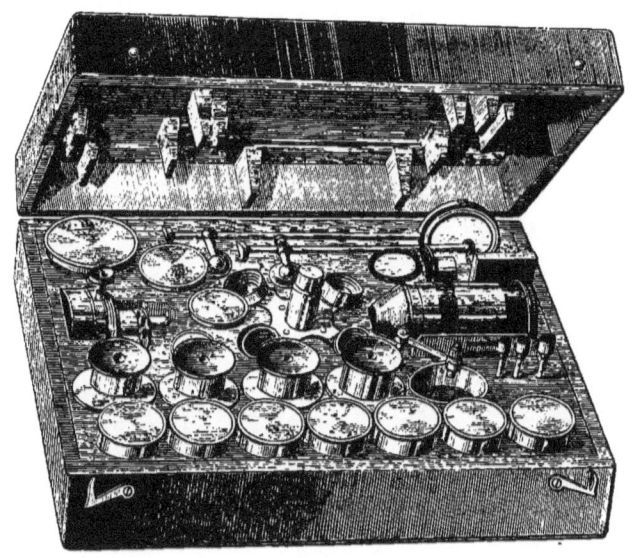

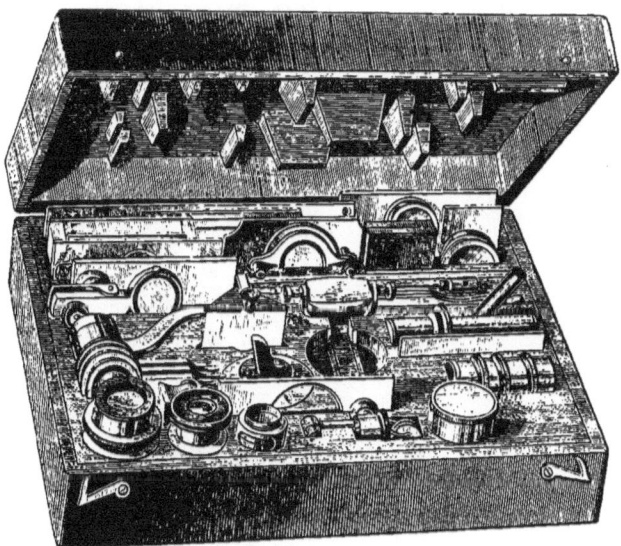

⅓rd scale.

Description of Plate XXVII.

Fig. 1. The flat mahogany case in which the Second-class Microscopes and apparatus are usually packed. No part of the Stand has to be taken to pieces when placed in the case, which is sufficiently large to receive the instrument and the most complete set of apparatus.

Fig. 2. A neatly framed wooden Stand, covered with leather on the top, which is sufficiently large to allow a Microscope and Lamp to be placed upon it. The stand is provided beneath with carefully made casters; so that it can be pushed about in any direction, upon an ordinary table, at which several persons may be seated; in this way the microscope may be passed from one person to another, without any alteration in the adjustment of the instrument, or any interchange of seats.

PLATE XXVII.

FIG. 1.

⅓rd scale.

FIG. 2.

¼th scale.

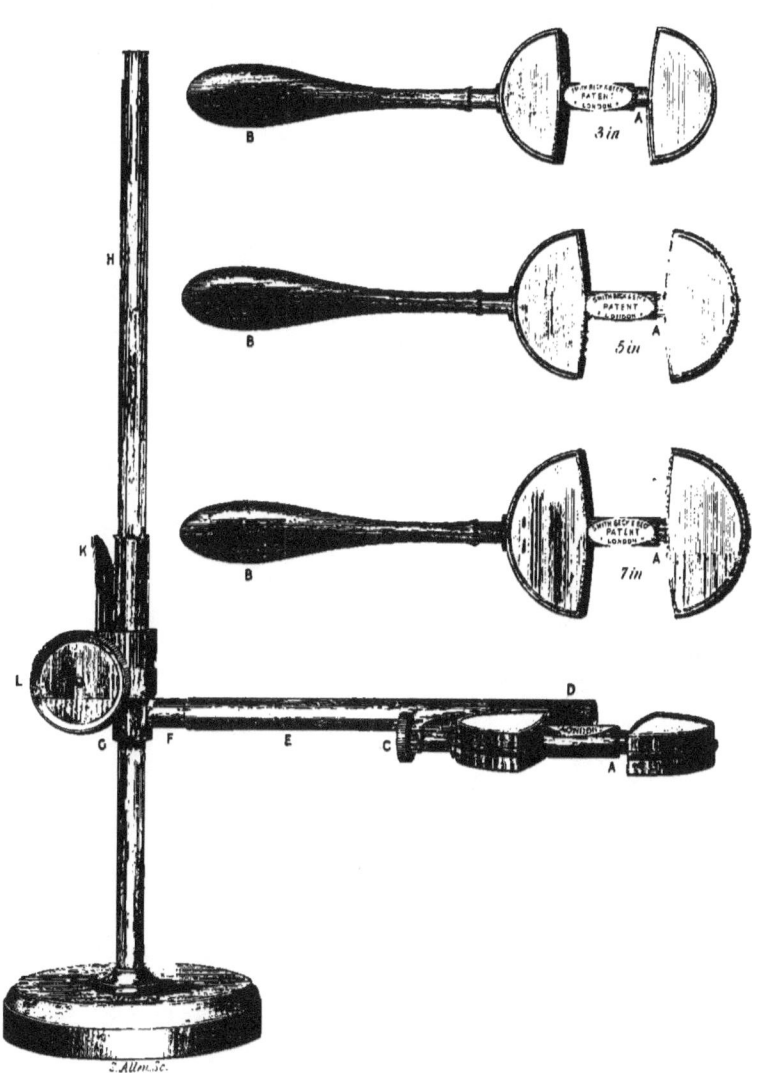

CATALOGUES, ETC.
PUBLISHED BY SMITH, BECK, AND BECK,
31, CORNHILL.

Price 6d. each.

ILLUSTRATED DESCRIPTION OF THE POPULAR MICROSCOPE.
ILLUSTRATED DESCRIPTION OF THE EDUCATIONAL MICROSCOPE.
ILLUSTRATED DESCRIPTION OF THE UNIVERSAL MICROSCOPE.

Scientific Catalogue of Microscopic Preparations.
Price 6d. each.

PART 1. VEGETABLE.
PART 2. BONES, TEETH, CARTILAGES, HAIRS, AND FEATHERS.
PART 3. ENTOMOLOGICAL.

Price 6d.

GENERAL CATALOGUE OF ACHROMATIC MICROSCOPES, ETC.—DESCRIPTION OF WENHAM'S BINOCULAR MICROSCOPE.—ILLUSTRATED DESCRIPTION OF THE PATENT BINOCULAR MAGNIFIERS.—ILLUSTRATED DESCRIPTION OF THE ACHROMATIC TABLE AND PATENT MIRROR STEREOSCOPES.

Price 2s. 6d.

ILLUSTRATED CATALOGUE OF SCIENTIFIC INSTRUMENTS.

PART II.

METEOROLOGICAL INSTRUMENTS.

Will be published early in April.
Price 2s. 6d.

ILLUSTRATED CATALOGUE OF SCIENTIFIC INSTRUMENTS.

PART I.

MICROSCOPES, AND APPARATUS, INSTRUMENTS USED IN PREPARING OBJECTS, MATERIALS USED IN MOUNTING OBJECTS, CABINETS, LAMPS, TABLES, ETC.

www.ingramcontent.com/pod-product-compliance
Lightning Source LLC
Chambersburg PA
CBHW032146230426
43672CB00011B/2469